DANCING AT THE WAFFLE HOUSE
and other stories Neal Boortz wishes he had told

**by
Angela K. Durden**

Dancing at the Waffle House

Dancing at the Waffle House

© 2018 Angela K. Durden

This publication is in the respected genre of humorous opinion such as produced by Will Rogers, Mark Twain, Charles Krauthammer, and others. Any reference to private individuals is done anonymously unless permissions were granted. Public figures are fair game.

This publication may not be reproduced, stored in a retrieval system, or transmitted in whole or in part, in any form, or by any means, electronic, mechanical, photocopying, recording, or otherwise, without the prior written permission of Angela K. Durden.
For permissions, write:

Blue Room Books
Attn: Permissions for Dancing at the Waffle House
2425 Lawrenceville Highway #C7, Decatur, GA 30033

Short quotations may be used by newspapers, magazines, and other publications, and online blogs as part of reviews, articles, or reports, but must attribute author and book title.

Editor: Tom Whitfield

Cover design and interior layout: Angela K. Durden
© 2018 Angela K. Durden | www.angeladurden.com

ISBN-13: 978-0-9854623-3-8
ISBN-10: 0-9854623-3-7 (Reference only)

Dancing at the Waffle House

DANCING AT THE WAFFLE HOUSE
© 2018 All Rights Reserved
978-0-9854623-3-8
Imprint: Blue Room Books
Angela K. Durden
angeladurden@msn.com

Dancing at the Waffle House

**BUSINESS BOOKS
by ANGELA K. DURDEN:**
Nine Stupid Things People do to Mess Up
Their Resumés (2000)

MEN! K.I.S.S. Your Resumé and Say Hello
to a Better Job (2013)
Also available as audio from Audible

LADIES! K.I.S.S. Your Resumé and Say
Hello to a Better Job (2013)

Opportunity Meets Motivation (2010)

Navigating the New Music Business as a
DIY and Indie: Coming Clean with the
Down and Dirty (2015)

CHILDREN'S BOOKS by AKD:
A Mike and His Grandpa Series:
Heroes Need Practice, Too! (2006)
The Balloon That Would Not Pop! (2012)

Dancing at the Waffle House

OTHER BOOKS by AKD:

Eloise Forgets How to Laugh (2010)
Twinkle, a memoir (2015)
First Time for Everything (2018)
Do Not Mistake This Smile (2018)

FICTION by DURDEN KELL:
Whitfield, Nebraska (2015)

**TWO NOVEL SERIES
IN DEVELOPMENT:
The Case Files of Smith and Jones:**
The Case of the Cotton Fiber Snuff Tape
The Case of the Cat-Loving Killer
The Case of the Angelic Assassin

The Dance Floor Wars:
Dispatches from the Front
Lucinda's People
Collisions
Life Cycle of a Fling

Dancing at the Waffle House

This book has been dedicated to…
well now, wouldn't you
like to know.

Dancing at the Waffle House

STOP!

DO NOT READ THIS BOOK IF YOU SELF-IDENTIFY AS A MEMBER OF THE PERPETUALLY OFFENDED GROUP — Pussy-Hat Wearing Politically Correct Democrat Liberal RINO Socialist Fascist Commies, otherwise known as P-HWPCDLRSFC throughout this book. By reading this book of opinions, you hereby swear you have not self-identified as a member of that group and/or if you are a member of that group, you agree to waive your rights to sue the publisher, the author and/or her children and/or estate, any and/or all bookstores and/or street vendors and/or libraries and/or any friend or relative of yours or mine who are selling or otherwise providing a copy of this book [EX.: you receive it as a gift]. If you read this book, whether or not you bought it, and if your feelings get hurt upon that reading, it will be clear you ignored the awesomely designed graphic containing a clear TRIGGER WARNING FOR THE PERPETUALLY OFFENDED included on the cover and on the first page of this book, and chose, AT YOUR OWN DISCRETION, to give up those rights and any and all recourse at law for getting a monetary settlement of any kind, including a refund for the purchase price, as the publisher believes in the concept of 01100010 01110101 01111001 01100101 01110010 00100000 01100010 01100101 01110111 01100001 01110010 01100101.

Contents, Table of

Getting Political.

11 Tetherball: My first brush with Socialism.
15 "Trump Anxiety" brings Kumbaya moments for everybody.
19 Are J. Brien and his paymasters dirty as hell?
23 Categorically opposed to a First-World problem.

Tech-No-RAM-O, or Up Yours, Citizens.

29 Snopes.com: Who can we believe in this story?
33 "Go, Indie!" Bezos would have liked that phrase at one time.
35 Facebook's newest secret app: Time Travel Portal.
41 Gutting the Constitution: The Myth of Net Neutrality.
47 Facebook says $100,000 in ads from troll farm made Hillary lose election.

An Important Message from the #CrunkNewsNetwork and other fake news outlets.

55 Crunk News Network: Delivering Jihad Justice.
61 The Rise of Citizen Journalists: A response to America's Media Meltdown.
69 Eclipse Sales Pitch: Wham! Bam! Thank you, Ma'am! Or, Why #CrunkNewsNetwork is still in business.

The Psychosis of the Politically Correct

75 United Network Command for Law and Enforcement.
79 Socialist public schools punish victims, reward bullies.
81 And therein lies the problem.
83 See Something, Say Something.

Dancing at the Waffle House

87   Cowboys and Indians and Posers.
91   You want I should go naked?
97   The Politics of Boobs.

Opinion, Varied
103   Dancing at the Waffle House.
105   Living life *tempo rubato*.
111   If I self-identify as a Female Native-American Caribbean-African Disabled Male Machinist HB1/2 Righty-Tighty-Lefty-Loosey Author, will my books sell faster?
115   "If I had a Hammer": The Terrorist Version.
117   Networked Fourth Estate: Citizen Journalists Carry the Torch.
123   The New War on Women is a War on Real Men: The New PC Power Grab.
127   Puddles, Negan, Dragoncon, and my failure to serve you well as Citizen Journalist.
131   The smaller the stakes, the fiercer the fight.
137   Angela answers job interview questions from hell.
145   No sense of humor at all: Bruce and Caitlyn bathroom doors.
151   Fads and Fashion and Fat…Oh, brother.

Other People
157   A Jazz Musician's OODA Loop.
161   He who would not be fooled: Baby Doll is not amused.
165   Numbers.
167   Liberals* are no fun, or The Case of T— and J. Brien.
171   Lido Pimienta generates fake racism event so she doesn't have to pay for column inches.
175   Galileo Galilei: Dissing God or unmasking gods?
Back Matter That Matters

Dancing at the Waffle House

Commencing to initiate to start to begin the book.

This is your last opportunity to
heed the Trigger Warning.
Do not say you haven't
been warned.

Dancing at the Waffle House

Dancing at the Waffle House

Neal Boortz and I go back a long time. It's not bragging if it's a fact, and the fact is we go back a *long* time — at least to 1990.

Do not mistake what I am saying.

That we go way back in no way implies Neal knows I exist because he does not — unless he happens to remember how I insulted him that one time on the air (something about astronauts and two paper bags), and did it so wittily, Southern charm intact, that he laughed snot bubbles and was left one-hundred percent speechless for the rest of his show, and to avoid dead air, they had to run two hours of "The Best of Boortz" because I slayed him.

Or if he happens to remember 'twas I who gave Royal Marshall the idea for recording callers' laughs and stringing them together, and Royal, little booger that he was, recorded *my* laugh while I was still on the air, then strung it together and ran it for a couple of weeks in a tour de force of marketing genius.

My laugh and Royal's editing genius got folks' attention. I know this for a fact because friends called me constantly and said, "Angela, Royal is playing your laugh — again! Wow, you and Neal must be good friends."

Dancing at the Waffle House

I miss Royal; his sudden death hurt many; I cried. Neal, I miss not so much. I'm kidding, Neal. *"Love you long time, five dollah!"*

For those who don't know, Boortz had a long-running radio talk show out of Atlanta. Sean Hannity, Herman Cain, Nancy Grace, and more than I can name or remember filled in for Neal, cutting or sharpening their on-air chops at the feet of the Talk Master before they went on to their own fame — or notoriety like former Atlanta Mayor Bill Campbell, who ended up doing prison time.

Therefore, when I had to come up with a name for this book, the first thing that popped out of my brain was a combination of two of my favorite things: Waffle House and Boortz.

They go together much like a chocolate martini goes with a hot serving of hash browns fresh from the grill — scattered well, covered, chunked, topped, and peppered.

That is to say: Very nicely. Or as my Uncle George (by marriage) used to say, "That's *choice*."

When Neal reads this book he will be so, so, so jealous. He's going to swoon in front of Donna, his long-suffering wife, and say, "Why, oh why, didn't I think of this? Imagine my fame if only I had. Damn her. However, since she is The Most Brilliant

Dancing at the Waffle House

Woman In The World, it's no wonder she thought of all this first."

Neal will approve of the contents because they are politically incorrect, pull no punches, are unafraid to get smarmy when needed, call it like it is, and take all credit for everything.

I say "Neal *will* approve" as if he hasn't already approved the contents because, as of the writing of this passage, he has not formally recognized their existence. He hasn't even seen the book, but I know he would sanction it, as in approve of every syllable, should he ever lay eyes on. Therefore, to my mind at least, he has as good as endorsed the book, so you might as well go ahead and buy it because Neal is telling you to.

And, since Neal often offended callers who chose to open their mouths and spout ill-formed and silly opinions, that class of buyer who would benefit from reading the words of The Most Brilliant Woman In The World would include all Pussy-Hat Wearing Politically Correct Democrat Liberal RINO Socialist Fascist Commies who continued to listen to Neal's show because they obviously like abuse.

It follows that if they called Neal, they will find plenty to feel abused about in this book and will want to read it.

Dancing at the Waffle House

If each P-HWPCDLRSFC [See pg. viii] would buy a copy, then go on social media and complain about it like they complained about Boortz, I would be most grateful. Just make sure you get my name spelled correctly. That would be A.N.G.E. — well, you can see it on the cover.

Neal's a busy man these days. Hard to get hold of. Busy, busy, busy, traveling around, so thoroughly acting the big shot retired popular talk show host that he has downright forgotten about me. How is that possible?

Have I forgotten about him?

I. Have. NOT!

Does he even call?

He. Does. NOT!

But do I still honor him by giving him free advertising by putting his name on the cover of my book and mentioning him liberally?

Yes. I. DO!

Which only goes to show you how humble I am, and proves Neal's opinion of me, namely that I am The Most Brilliant Woman In The World.

Sincerely,

AKD.
In her lonely writer's garret
early on the day of July 4, 2018

Dancing at the Waffle House

Dancing at the Waffle House

Getting Political

But not how one usually
thinks of getting political.

Dancing at the Waffle House

Tetherball: My first brush with Socialism.

Sixth Grade. East Point, Georgia. Church Street Elementary. The year was...well, never mind. Suffice it to say, I had my first brush with Socialism, though I didn't know what that was. But it became clear quite fast that me and it would never get along. In one way or another since then, I've fought against it with vigor. Here's the story.

Miss Chapman introduces her class to this new sport called tetherball. A ball on a rope is attached to a pole. Two people smack the ball in opposing directions, each attempting to wrap the rope around the pole until there is no more rope left. The person who wraps all the way first is declared the winner of that match.

Miss Chapman tells us that whoever wins the match will play until he loses. Simple enough. Sounded fair. Everybody agreed it was an awesome concept.

One-on-one play.

Mano a mano.

You will have to read my book *Twinkle, a memoir* to discover why I was always the new girl in class. This year of sixth grade was no different. It had been a tougher than normal year at home and at school during fifth grade. Then over the summer we moved yet again and there I am: New Girl. Again. Mother was in the process of leaving forever her abusive second husband for about the gabillionth time only to return two days later because she missed him very much.

Unneeded drama was nonstop. I was mad.

Little wonder I took joy where it could be found.

So, there I am. Taking joy as I wait my turn to test myself one-to-one against an individual. I step up and within a few smacks of the ball, I had won the match.

Yay! Bring on the next contestant.

I win again. The record to beat was three wins in a row. Up steps the next player. I win again, making me and a boy tied for first place in consecutive wins.

So far, so good. I continue to beat the pants off everybody that steps up. I was fierce but ladylike. That is, I hit that ball like a gladiator, but my dress never raised enough to show my panties.

After beating well over half the class, intent in my mission to win, I was vaguely aware that applause and shouts of "Go, go, go Angela" had stopped. Everything around me got still as I won yet again.

Dancing at the Waffle House

Our teacher stepped toward me. Miss Chapman, a wonderful teacher I dearly loved, then spoke.

"Angela, you've won enough. It's time to let somebody else win." My fellow students nodded their heads in agreement. I looked from them to the teacher.

Thus began my first brush with Socialism.

Foretelling the path my life would take, my response was swift and immediate. Horrified, and more than a little disappointed, I yelled, "You want me to *lose on purpose?*"

Miss Chapman, bless her heart, did not want that. But she had a group of malcontents getting ready to riot because it simply wasn't fair that Angela was winning that much. If Angela could simply cede the throne, Miss Chapman's problem would be solved and everybody else could have a turn.

Make it all equal. Walk away.

Nobody gets hurt.

Incensed, I said, "Everybody *is* playing! You said winner plays until they lose. I can't help it they don't know how to play the game. Let them beat me. You want me to *quit?*"

I was beyond furious.

Dancing at the Waffle House

Miss Chapman saw this conversation was not going to get better; she pretty much ordered me to step away from the pole. Which I did, but not happily, and I refused to play that game with them ever again.

"Trump Anxiety" brings kumbaya moments for everybody.

Kumbaya, my Lord. The old spiritual was written during the Roaring Twenties. The official version was sung in Gullah and called *Come by Yuh*. Everybody knows it — or knows of it. These days "kumbaya" is used as a snarky comment or a call for a group hug. Flexibility is its strong point. The song is a repetition of a simple melodic line and barely changing lyrics consisting of:

Kumbaya my Lord, kumbaya (sung 3x)
Someone's [singing, laughing, crying, praying, sleeping] Lord, kumbaya (sung 3x each)
Each section followed by: Oh Lord, kumbaya

Trump campaign promise — Job Creation: Hell, yeah; promise kept.

Job Creation has put certain pastors and therapists in paradise because of the current worrisome political climate, something they have named "Trump Anxiety".

Dancing at the Waffle House

More are seeing their parishioners and clients exhibit signs of "Trump Anxiety", leading to public meltdowns such as this woman who wrote on her Facebook page:

I actually had a very long and vivid dream the other night about him, and what made it a nightmare was that I had to be his babysitter/keeper. He was at times a self-centered five-year-old in a man's body, unable to sit still, listen, behave, or focus on anything but himself. I really did have this dream. Really.

We really do believe you, lady. Really.

Quoted on baptistnews.com, after mentioning a "very stable man" who had a meltdown in a meeting:

"It reminds me how brittle people really are," said Julie Pennington-Russell, senior pastor at First Baptist Church in Washington, D.C. "We are in that kind of time when churches have so much to offer.
"As much as ever, churches have a beautiful opportunity right now to reach people who otherwise wouldn't think of reaching for God." Further, she added, "We must keep grounding our congregants and ourselves in what is not shakeable."

Dancing at the Waffle House

And from his Facebook page, an Atlanta therapist said:

I would be glad to see people who are suffering from anxiety and depression, or other concerns related to the current political and cultural situation.

Who's hitching up their gitalong? See? Job creation centered around kumbaya moments. Trump has thought of you, no matter if you are singing, laughing, crying, or praying.

Of course, I believe the majority having crying meltdowns are Pussy-Hat Wearing Politically Correct Democrat Liberal RINO Socialist Fascist Commies watching their dreams die. See, the P-HWPCDLRSFC [See pg. viii] have lived in fairy tale land for such a long time they assumed their lives would always be this way.

But God loves them, too. I know this because the Bible tells me so, right?

Anyway, for those of us who have been living in the real world and praying, we're not having any meltdown in this current political and cultural climate. Folks have been fighting it since The Sixties when radical professors took over the campuses with unscrupulous power grabs.

Dancing at the Waffle House

Heck, we'd have already been "back in the USSR" if we hadn't been #standingfirm against those power grabs.

We're the ones putting on our boots, hitching up our gitalongs, pushing them recalcitrant P-HWPCDLRSFC [See pg. viii] dogies, and hollering "Gitterdun, Hammer, gitterdun!"

Are J. Brien and his paymasters dirty as hell?

I do not claim to be an attorney. However, from reading the memorandum and order, it seems to me that when Trump said he was being secretly recorded, he was not lying. The order from the court seems to show that the US Government, for over a year, was already deploying a software-based listening/recording device *without a court order.*

And that when the agents got their fingers caught in the cookie jar, they then attempted to get the phone provider to do the tapping for them *without a court order because J. Brien Comey said it was all right to do it, and he didn't mind if they would get on with it.*

Stopping what some allege was Obama's illegal order to the FBI, thankfully the phone provider refused J. Brien's request, forcing the US Government to try to get a lawful court order that would compel the phone company to bug Trump and his environs.

Here is the main summary of the court's memorandum:

Dancing at the Waffle House

Until recently, the agents consensually monitored the Subject Telephone's communications and location by using "a software-based solution" that did not require the Provider's participation…. The government reports that the latter product was recently "discontinued" without explaining how that discontinuance renders the product it was already using ineffective (although I assume that it must be so).

The government does not discuss whether any alternative products or services are available, or whether there is any other way for it to engage in the consensual monitoring of a person's telephone communications without requiring the Provider to install a wiretap. Instead, it simply reports the discontinuance of one product and then writes: "Thus, the government is requesting this proposed Order…."

The Provider is unwilling to install the wiretap the government seeks without a court order….

Given that refusal, the government posits, "a Court order is necessary." The government proposes that if its request is granted, it will instruct its agents "that they may intercept and record communications over the SUBJECT TELEPHONE only in accordance with 18 USC. § 2511(2)(c), i.e., that they may intercept and record only those calls (or portions of calls) over the SUBJECT TELEPHONE in which the [Witness] is personally involved as a party to the communication...."

In layman's terms the above means this:

FBI said "Sir, yes, Sir" to Obama's order for an illegal wiretap.
When CYA efforts went into effect, telecom company said, "Hell no, we ain't doing that as a favor. You got to give us lawful court order. Oh, and by the way, how dare you illegally wiretap our lines."
FBI said, "Oh yeah, we're going to make you do it anyway so nananabooboo."
Court said, "No. FBI can't make telecom snoop without providing proper legal proof. You got proper legal proof you need to do that? Yes? No?"

Of course, how the media is spinning this court order is that J. Brien Comey, the FBI's smartest Diewrecktoré, was doing God's work, so it doesn't matter that what the FBI did was illegal because it was needed to save the world from "The Hammer", damn it.
Wait a sec: Do Libs believe in God?

Dancing at the Waffle House

Categorically Opposed to a First-World Problem.

I can shovel dung out of a barn by the wheelbarrow load and never gag, but let me watch a commercial for a "new and revolutionary litter box" as they demonstrate the clumped sorting part, or see somebody with a little plastic bag bend over to pick up what their dog just dumped, and I'll retch projectile-fashion in a split nanosecond.

What to do with your dog's poo is literally a first-world problem. Who else picks up their dog's dropping, wraps it in plastic, carefully carries it to a trash can, and throws it away?

Nobody.

Even in France, everybody knows to watch where you place your tootsies because they let their dogs poo where they will, then casually walk on. Of course, tourists report Frenchies also don't use deodorant, so maybe using them as an example is…never mind. My logic has already broken down here. Moving on to what is most important in this narrative: Me.

Why do I have the two opposing reactions to the same by-product?

As you have surmised, I am The Most Brilliant Woman In The World. As such, I've given this topic a lot of thought and have concluded it has to do with the opposing concepts of Socialism vs. Capitalism.

I am a Capitalist and Capitalists are practical people.

They make money the old-fashioned way: They earn it. Cows earn their keep. Animals that perform — that is, what they do will sell a ticket — also earn their keep. Young, second wives of rich men earn their keep.

See? All Capitalists.

Pets, on the other hand, are Socialists waiting on Big Gubment to cater to their every whim and fancy. The concept of earning their keep is not part of the equation. All they need do is wag their tail, purr, or squawk, things they would normally do even if nobody is watching, and — WHAM! — "Does Muffie want a new toy? Yes, Muffie wants a new toy. Oh, no. Muffie doesn't like her new toy? I'm so sorry, Muffie. Let me remove it from your sight and get you another one."

See? Socialists all.

Therefore, since I am categorically opposed to Socialism and it makes me gag, my gag reflex to pet poo makes perfect sense.

And yet the same first-worlders who dutifully follow their pets picking up poo are the same people who say nothing at all about the wolves, foxes, and coyotes living nearby who dump their poo — willy-nilly — throughout pristine wildlife sanctuaries, maybe even on top of nests of the rare Ground-dwelling Crusted Piealamode Whistling NutterButter Sammich Whoopie, and late at night in neighboring yards after feasting on cats and kittens and puppies.

Frankly, I'm surprised Socialists have not used government job creation programs to hire people with plastic bags to follow these wild dog types around, and also to study and document the exact nature of the impact to the environment in order to determine what other vast funds could be diverted to the elite group of caring P-HWPCDLRSFCs' [See pg. viii] overreaching but much-needed solution to the problem.

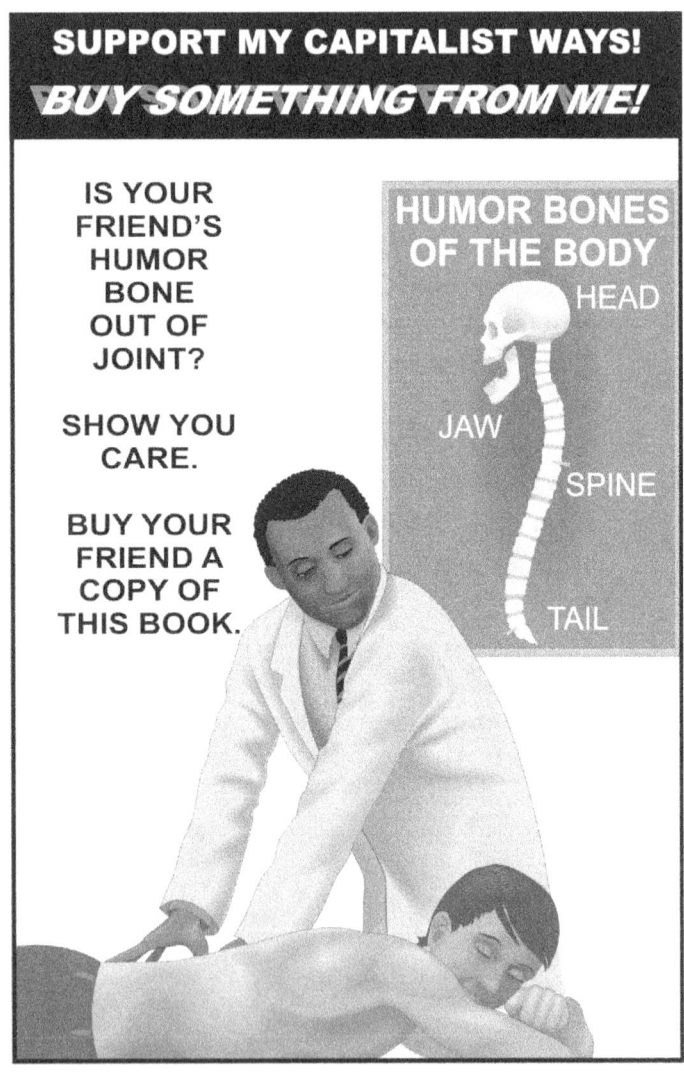

Dancing at the Waffle House

Tech-no-Ram-O, or Up yours, Citizens.

Dear Tech User Slave,
 01100110 01110101 01100011 01101011 00100000 01111001 01101111 01110101 00100000 01100001 01101110 01100100 00100000 01110100 01101000 01100101 00100000 01101000 01101111 01110010 01110011 01100101 00100000 01111001 01101111 01110101 00100000 01110010 01101111 01100100 01100101 00100000 01101001 01101110 00100000 01101111 01101110.

Sincerely,
Tech Giants

Dancing at the Waffle House

Snopes.com: Who can we believe in this story?

While I rake the Mainstream Media (MSM) over the coals on a regular basis when they abuse their power, I equally give kudos when I read a truly fair and balanced story.

Daniel Victor in The New York Times wrote such an article about the woes of Snopes.com, a popular site that gives thumbs up or down to the truthfulness of news stories.

Here's what is going on with Snopes.com. Basically, a co-founder is being shoved out of his own company. It's turning messy, as these things often do, because that co-founder pitches a hissy fit when he is asked to act responsibly with the money. Not all founders end up being pushed out of companies they start, but usually when it does happen it's because the founder does not have the skill set to handle new challenges of a growing company. In other words, he is still playing loosey-goosey with the cash register.

Call me a contrarian, but I stopped paying attention to Snopes.com some years ago when I found that even their so-called unbiased and learned opinions weren't so unbiased and often were unlearned. When I found out Facebook had chosen them as one of their verified fact checkers to determine if a story was real, the funeral was over.

I once contacted Snopes.com via their website so I could interview them. They didn't get back to me. Oh, they will talk to the venerable Gray Lady, as The New York Times is often called, but a Citizen Journalist? Oh, no; not one of their ilk. Not someone without properly authorized press credentials.

Who is Angela K. Durden that Snopes.com should deign to be interviewed by her? I've got a middle initial and everything, but does Snopes care? No, they do not.

For a company that holds others to a high standard of clarity, Snopes.com hides far too much about themselves, as you can see from this whois.icann.org screenshot:

Dancing at the Waffle House

ICANN WHOIS

snopes.com

Lookup

Showing results for: SNOPES.COM
Original Query: snopes.com

Contact Information

Registrant Contact
Name: PERFECT PRIVACY, LLC
Organization:
Mailing Address: 12808 Gran Bay Parkway West, Jacksonville FL 32258 US
Phone: +1.5707088780
Ext:
Fax:
Fax Ext:
Email: k35xv54a3vv@networksolutionsprivateregistration.com

Admin Contact
Name: PERFECT PRIVACY, LLC
Organization:
Mailing Address: 12808 Gran Bay Parkway West, Jacksonville FL 32258 US
Phone: +1.5707088780
Ext:
Fax:
Fax Ext:
Email: k35xv54a3vv@networksolutionsprivateregistration.com

Tech Contact
Name: PERFECT PRIVACY, LLC
Organization:
Mailing Address: 12808 Gran Bay Parkway West, Jacksonville FL 32258 US
Phone: +1.5707088780
Ext:
Fax:
Fax Ext:
Email: k35xv54a3vv@networksolutionsprivateregistration.com

Dancing at the Waffle House

Granted, there are plenty who hide their physical location, and there is no law mandating disclosure, but Snopes should not be one of those who hide because they are all about open and clear.

But they aren't, are they?

The co-founder's court case is forcing the inner workings of that company out in the open. When my friend, worried about losing an objective reporting site, read me the email he received wherein Snopes' co-founder asked for money to fight the big bad meanie corporation, I said that co-founder was spinning his own story.

Seems my objective research proved me right. Oh, Snopes, Snopes, Snopes. Go ahead and close your doors. You don't look good on life support.

Hmmmm...

I wonder. If I share this on Facebook, will it pass the Snopes-verified smell test?

"Go, Indie!" Bezos would have liked that phrase at one time.

The most current circulation numbers I could find predated Jeff Bezos buying The Washington Post. Can't seem to find any stats after the 2013 purchase by Nash Holdings, a company Bezos set up to acquire the paper. Up until that date, the numbers were declining quickly. Would it be too far off target to suggest the numbers for the print product are worse now? Probably not.

As if the newspaper business isn't chapping his backside enough, Amazon (which, rumor has it, has never made a profit) is pushing a price war to get sales volume up.

This is particularly disturbing to the Big 5 book publishers. Amazon is playing games with the book business. If you are an author published by one of the Big 5 or their subsidiaries, you will not be happy about Amazon's shenanigans.

Of course, as a small publisher, my sales volume does not put me in Bezos' gunsight. But I have to ask, "If many of the buttons consumers click are set by automated algorithms, who's to say I'm not losing out on sales, too?"

Independent bookstores are making a comeback. I know because I have one in my neighborhood I've been buying from for years. Business is picking up for Eagle Eye Bookstore. People like to talk to people. The owner, Doug Robinson, is president of SIBA, a trade association for indie bookstores.

At one time, Bezos would have appreciated the phrase "Go Indie!" Too bad Jeff wants to rule the world.

Jeff Bezos
(WikiCommons)

Facebook's newest secret app: Time Travel Portal.

For several years now, that giant of social engineering called Facebook has regularly let my followers and friends know where I am. They've done it without my permission, too. Not that I'm complaining, mind you.

Of course, Fake...errrrr...I mean Facebook is doing as great a job of it as they are in identifying fake news.

For instance, when I post to my Facebook timeline links to my columns on my blog, I'm always asked to confirm that it is really me who is posting by typing into a box a cryptic set of randomly generated letters.

Not that Fake...errrr...Facebook identified all the fake news headlines generating massive free publicity about them when it was erroneously reported they shut down the Baby Terminator, or the Smart Bot AI project.

Did you know that Facebook does not recognize many sites as legitimate? It's probably because one of their Fake News Identifier vendors has not put their stamp of approval somewhere in a database. This could be because Snopes.com is busy with infighting and purse-string-controlling lawsuits right now, but I'm only guessing.

Then again, maybe Facebook thinks I'm in the witness protection program or I need to hide from stalkers and they believe — in typical Big Brother fashion — they are being helpful by hiding my actual whereabouts.

This might not be a bad thing except I'm not and I don't.

In any case, for several years Facebook has regularly moved me to Oceanside, California. All of a sudden, my posts show I'm across the continent when an hour previous I was in Atlanta. No wonder people think I'm everywhere all the time.

There is no rhyme or reason to it, and I haven't been able to figure out what triggers it. Their doing this on my behalf has caused family strife as well. You see, I have a cousin who lives a mere 32 miles from Oceanside in Capistrano Beach who finally posted one day that she sure did have her feelings hurt because I was so close and didn't visit.

She got a good laugh when I explained about witness protection and such, but the other day Facebook topped itself with a secret rollout of its newest app. It is called the Time Travel Portal.

You read correctly: Time Travel Portal.

Dancing at the Waffle House

There I am, hosting one of the meetups for the Atlanta Songwriters Club at the famous Red Light Café in Midtown Atlanta. After getting the requisite photos to share with those who could not attend, I went to post these to our Facebook page, and that is when I found out I had been to China and back in less than four hours.

Not only that, the entire Red Light Café itself, forty attendees and the owners, all sponsors and my friends and their friends, the kitchen and bathrooms, fans and artwork, seating and tables, sound and lighting system, as well as instruments and my wine were transported as if we were all in a giant time machine.

I've got photographic proof from screenshots I took. Look if you dare. Look closely at the backward writing on the banner behind us. Look, I say, look! More proof we were on the other side of the world.

Dancing at the Waffle House

Proof that Facebook has a Time Travel Portal

Dancing at the Waffle House

See? You won't find any fake news in these pages. You learned it here first, folks. Citizen Journalist at your service.

Now it's time to go out and buy some of that Facebook stock because this Time Travel Portal app is going to take over the world. You might as well sell all your stocks in all airlines including Virgin, as well as the parent company of bus service Greyhound, taxi services Uber and Lyft, and UPS and FedEx.*

The day you are reading this I will be driving from Nashville in that great State of Tennessee to Blue Ridge, Georgia. Why am I driving, you ask?

Because thus far, Facebook's newest secret app, the Time Travel Portal (internal working name is That Thing That Makes Us Go, or T3), is not yet available because it is still secret, deployed as they deploy all their apps, that is to say, when they dang well feel like it and not when their stupid users need them.

Notice to #CrunkNewsNetwork and other MSM outlets:

I know you are trolling me for real news tips in order to make yourself look more legitimate and save your reputation, but you need to go out and find your own news. I shall not divulge my sources for this story. Na-na-na boo-boo to you, #CrunkNewsNetwork.

Dancing at the Waffle House

*LEGAL DISCLAIMER: Angela K. Durden is not a licensed stockbroker though she does have a driver's license and a carry permit, both issued by the great State of Georgia in the United States. Angela K. Durden neither endorses Facebook, nor any airline including Virgin, nor any bus or taxi service except for Donnie who drives a legally licensed taxi and is a fine fellow to boot, nor those Uber corporate creeps or Lyft, but she does endorse UPS as they are totally awesome and FedEx does a mighty fine job, too. By reading this column, you agree that Angela K. Durden has not officially told you to buy or sell any stock and that if you proceed to do so you will hold harmless Angela K. Durden, and her children, though you may sue her ex-husband if you can get any money out of his penny-pinching fingers...never mind, she digresses. And you acknowledge that you have enough brains to make your own financial decisions and do not need to rely for stock tips from a columnist who likes to occasionally write humorous content.

Gutting the Constitution: The Myth of Net Neutrality.

Remember Net Neutrality hype?

Remember when former US President Obama started pushing the concept of a free and open Internet as if it weren't already free and open?

Do you remember when the details of it were made known that it mostly amounted to another way for the government to control the Internet by controlling the companies providing connections to our homes?

Do you remember Obama wanted to classify providers as Public Utility Companies?

Do you remember how Google and other Tech Giants applauded the legislation and thought Obama was the best thing since Kleen Maid Sliced Bread?

Well, maybe you don't remember. But that's okay because your Citizen Journalist is here to remind you of it. And why should she be reminding you of it now? Because Donald "The Hammer" Trump is getting ready to, yet again, rescind an Obama ruling.

This has given the MSM opportunity to write articles bashing Trump, Tech Giants reason to worry, and prompted many on Facebook and Twitter (who have no clue) to pass around links to online petitions: *We Want Free Internet. Don't Take Our Free Internet.*

When Obama classified providers of broadband as utilities, he then put them under the control of Big Government. Bill Clinton fell for the same thing when he signed into being the Digital Millennium Copyright Act, or DMCA, that was out of date and completely useless one day after it was signed.

I'm all for law and order, but many laws are useless because of the way they are worded. Think about it. The DMCA and Net Neutrality are versions of old, silly laws like —

> "It is illegal to walk your crocodile without a leash along Main Street during a full moon while your ex-wife is visiting her mother to attend her father's funeral."

There is no law like that, but there are laws about walking your crocodile, and the DMCA and Net Neutrality rules were written over the top like that, making them completely useless and punishing, so you get my drift.

You might be asking, "Yes, Angela, but we want to be able to keep the Internet free and open to all. What if a website wants to be on the Internet but the broadband company says they can't be on it? I mean, really, Angela, isn't that just wrong?"

Maybe. Maybe not.

What does one mean by *free*?

Free, as in the right to publish what one wants? Or *free*, as in not paying for it? The first definition already has the Constitution governing that freedom. The latter is pie-in-the-sky thinking as nothing comes with no cost.

The US Government and Tech Giants are working hand-in-fist to limit Constitution-guaranteed freedoms. Net Neutrality is simply another way they are doing it.

By controlling the companies who bring connections to your house, the government has put themselves in control of your Internet access. That means politicians can shut it down whenever they want.

Tech Giants, playing the victim, push messaging such as this from Google, a statement that many other Tech Giants agree with:

"Our values remain the same: The Internet should be competitive and open. **That means no Internet access provider should block or degrade Internet traffic, nor should they sell 'fast lanes' that prioritize particular Internet services over others.** These rules should apply regardless of whether you're accessing the Internet using a cable connection, a wireless service, or any other technology."

Let's break down this self-serving statement, shall we?

What companies are the worst offenders when it comes to selling "fast lanes" that prioritize certain Internet services?

First on the list would be Goo-Goo-Goo...that's right. You've almost got the whole word out of your mouth. That company has formed a parent company called Alphabet that is working even harder behind the scenes to control what you see and when you see it.

How about Fakebook, as many popularly call that social media giant these days? Or Twitter or any of those other platforms you like so very much and want, yet are unable to function and live without?

Yes, they too control access within their silos and try their damnedest to keep you on their site by making big promises about your ability to freely share information — only to then break each one once they've got you hooked. Does Twitter's *shadow banning* sound familiar? Or how about Facebook *limiting* how many *friends* you can have, how many can see your posts in their feed, or severely limiting how many friends you can tell about events you're putting on?

Or Google's pushing of expensive and meaningless *HTTPS* certifications on all websites no matter what? Or not allowing AdWords to be used by a company working hard to protect intellectual property rights? Or favoring certain news sources to always show up in searches but all unapproved news sources to show up on page 134,567

Your access to the Internet has always been controlled. Nothing is free.

There is a cost to building the infrastructure. Do you know there are people who do not know that the Internet comes through a wire to their house? They think because they have Wi-Fi that somehow those bits and bytes magically appear. They think that a satellite magically delivers it, like a leprechaun grants a wish.

Hello! Everything is hard-wired somewhere. Satellite dishes in yards pick up signals, and wire brings it inside your house to a piece of hardware that connects to your computer and/or phone.

And you pay monthly for the convenience of that service delivered to your home. Stop paying the bill and you stop getting the service.

Dancing at the Waffle House

It is stupid for Tech Giants to act like their growth was not and is not dependent on *you paying your monthly bill for access to the Internet.*

But even Tech Giants are seeing the writing on the wall.

Why else does Goo-Goo-Goo spend massive amounts of money to make robo calls and send snail mail to small businesses about advertising with them? Remember what this is all about:

Keeping you from freedom.

Steve Jobs once said if you are not paying for the service, your data is the service.

Facebook says $100,000 in ads from troll farm made Hillary lose election.

PBS and NPR: Deaf.
Facebook: Blind.
Troll farms: Sneaky.
Clintons: Persecuted.

You know, there once was a time I was like most folks who listened to National Public Radio: I trusted them. But that changed, and I quit a few years back because I hate to vomit. NPR couldn't find its backside with GPS.

Not to say that I haven't heard some interesting things on their programs. For instance, that is where I heard the story about the Mojave Desert Phone Booth, which prompted me to write a song about it. This great song would not have existed had I not listened to NPR.

But those inspiring stories became fewer. I tired of waiting for more.

It became painful, and a waste of my time, slogging through the Pussy-Hat Wearing Politically Correct Democratic Socialist Liberal RINO Fascist Commie talking points to get to something that might be relevant to an independent-minded person.

On their website, NPR boasts of winning hundreds of awards, many from prestigious journalism organizations, while they say of themselves:

"On-air and online, NPR presents fact-based, independent journalism that examines and airs diverse perspectives. NPR's journalists strive for mastery of the narrative form, telling stories in ways that transport the audience to the places where news is happening and introducing the people affected."

Doesn't that sound lofty and worthy and caring? Of course it does. But how independent can NPR be when the stories are the same as everybody else's in mainstream media where narrow views produce narrow storylines? Storylines, by the way, that always give institutionalized evil a pass.

In 2011 NPR took money from George Soros' foundation. To explain it, they said:

"...But the organization made a judgment last fall that taps into that credibility account. The decision was to take $1.8 million from the Open Society Foundations. It's funded by left-leaning billionaire financier-philanthropist George Soros, who made his fortune in hedge funds and currency speculation. ***The money is for a worthy purpose..."***

With sarcasm fully intact, I say: Of course it is, sweeties. See? NPR knew Soros was — let me chuckle a moment at the understatement — left-leaning, but they took the money anyway.

I went to NPR's website and searched for that worthy purpose. It is called Impact of Government, and also Impact on Government. Which are two completely different titles.

Supposedly they were going to have two stringers in each state who would focus on state politics that often do not get covered in the media. Here's what I found they did for $1.8 million.

Dancing at the Waffle House

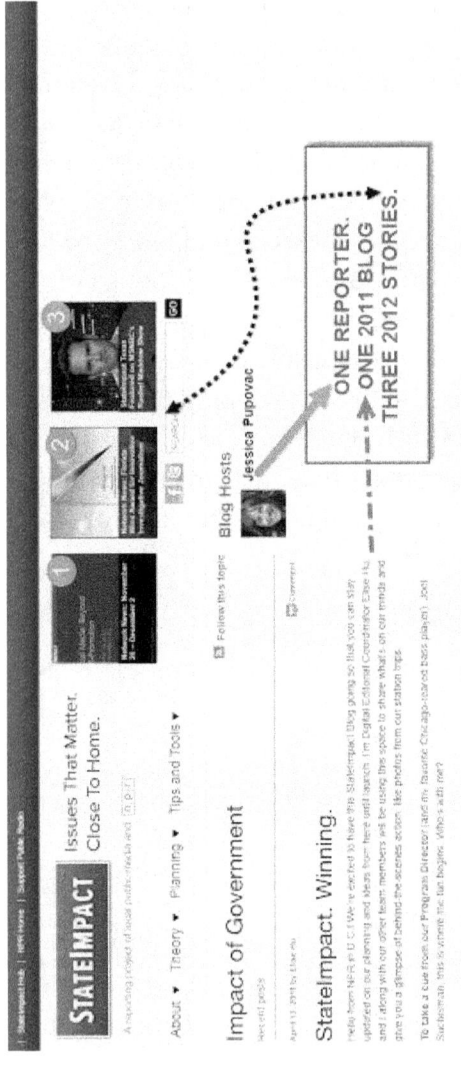

Dancing at the Waffle House

And nothing since. Hey, Soros? I'll write for that kind of money. Oh, wait. I already write, and I do it at my own expense as a Citizen Journalist.

Now NPR is reporting that social media giant Facebook, the sharing bastion of caring around the world and self-appointed watchdog of fake news, says that $100,000 they made selling ads on their portal to a troll farm in Florida made Hillary lose.

And they say it with a straight face?

I'd laugh except it isn't funny.

Dancing at the Waffle House

An important message from the #CrunkNewsNetwork and other fake news outlets

Dear Reader/Viewer,

You are getting SLEEEEpeeee. Hear us:
You are wrong and stupid and have mush for brains. We are right, smart, and know what is best for you. Put down this book and buy our newspapers and magazines and watch our broadcasts. PUHLEEZE!

Sincerely, the MSM

Dancing at the Waffle House

Crunk News Network: Delivering Jihad Justice 24/7.

In 2017, a young fellow put together a meme of Donald "The Hammer" Trump from his days of appearing on professional wrestling shows and made it currently socially relevant (and absolutely entertaining) by pasting a CNN logo over the head of another guy near the ring. "President Hammer" thought the CNN logo getting pounded by him was so funny that he had his people add sound and retweet it.

Can you say "Go Viral!" five times real fast? The young man could and found that a reason to celebrate.

Until...

Until, that is, CNN — or Crunk News Network* — went after the boy, barrels blazing:

Dancing at the Waffle House

After posting his apology, "HanA**holeSolo" called CNN's KFile and confirmed his identity. In the interview, HanA**holeSolo sounded nervous about his identity being revealed and asked to not be named out of fear for his personal safety and for the public embarrassment it would bring to him and his family.

CNN is not publishing "HanA**holeSolo's" name because he is a private citizen who has issued an extensive statement of apology, showed his remorse by saying he has taken down all his offending posts, and because he said he is not going to repeat this ugly behavior on social media again. In addition, he said his statement could serve as an example to others not to do the same.

CNN reserves the right to publish his identity should any of that change.

CRUNK NEWS NETWORK:

THE MOST FEARED NAME IN NEWS.

Dancing at the Waffle House

#CNNBlackmail

What creeps. What bullies.

Yes, ladies and gentlemen, Crunk News Network — whose proposed new taglines are ***Delivering Jihad Justice 24/7*** or ***Do What We Say or Else You're Going to Get It*** — themselves put the smackdown on one Citizen Journalist who used the time-honored method of social commentary called "humor". They went full Charlie Hebdo on the young man.

Crunk News Network knows what that attack style looks like, seeing as how in 2015 the network did a full timeline report on Justice Delivered Jihad Style. Remember the Charlie Hebdo attack?

Charlie Hebdo is a French satirical weekly newspaper. Featuring cartoons, reports, polemics, and jokes, the publication is cheeky, bold, and loudly non-conformist. Intensely secular, anti-religious, and left-wing, they mock everybody including Catholicism, Judaism, Islam, and a wide variety of other groups as local and world news develops.

In 2006, Islamic organizations sued over the publishing of a likeness of Muhammad — and lost. Al-Qaeda added Charlie Hebdo editor-in-chief and cartoonist Stéphane "Charb"

Dancing at the Waffle House

Charbonnier to its most wanted list. Charb replied, "We have to carry on until Islam has been rendered as banal as Catholicism." He applied for a permit to carry a firearm for self-defense, but never got permission.

Naturally the next logical move was for Al-Qaeda simply to fire-bomb the Charlie Hebdo office and murder Charbonnier. So they did.

CNN waged jihad on this young man who made the Trump-CNN meme, so CNN cannot say they don't believe in Holy War. Not when they put the boy on their most wanted list, issued their own fatwa against him, then sent their MSM buddies on an unrelenting and persecutorial campaign.

CNN should be absolutely ashamed and contrite. ***But they aren't.***

CNN should apologize to that kid, and to all citizens. ***But they won't.***

They are proud of what they did to this young man and, by extension, to all citizens of the world. Yes, the world. Because freedom of expression, free speech, the right to speak freely, has been trampled again.

That CNN stomped on constitutional rights publicly shows they've got the big head and

Dancing at the Waffle House

that they're so scared of the power of Citizen Journalists they're wetting their pants.

*Crunk News Network's committees and advertising agencies — both full of movers and shakers and important and very smart people — are studying polling data from focus groups to determine which tagline will work best with their core demographics, that is to say, Socialists and Terrorists.

So far, the taglines' popularity ratings are in a dead heat. **Internal memos from anonymous sources within the network** say the solution will be revolutionary: Crunk News Network is thinking of using both taglines, rotating their usage in 24-hour cycles.

Another source supplied a sneak peek at one tagline's artwork but refused to speak on the record, that is to say they remain a publicly unknown but privately highly trustworthy source, who said, "They would simply *kill* me if they knew I was the one who stole their rollout thunder, so please don't tell them my name. I've got kids, you know."**

Anyway, the ad agency felt the network should pay homage to all those who came before. As you can see, they have done that in the logo on the following page. Pol Pot and the Khmer Rouge. Hitler and the SS. ISIS and Jihadi Jane. What's not to love?

Dancing at the Waffle House

** We reserve the right to publish our source's identity if she/he/it changes her/his/its mind.

The Rise of Citizen Journalists: A response to America's Media Meltdown.

Victor Davis Hanson writes brilliantly and bluntly about America's Media Meltdown. Here is a quote from his article on Hoover.org:

"Obama himself channeled the veneration, variously promising in god-like fashion to cool the planet and lower the seas, remarking that his own multifaceted expertise was greater than that of all of the various specialists who ran his campaign. For the next eight years, the media largely ignored what might charitably be called an historic overextension of presidential power and scandal not seen since the days of Richard Nixon's presidency. A clique of journalists set up a private chat group, JournoList, through which they could channel ideas to promote the Obama progressive agenda."

Dancing at the Waffle House

Hanson (pictured here) has done a fine job of explaining how and why the media rabidly worship at the feet of their P.C. messiah as they continue to proclaim him the only hope for mankind while conversely demonizing his successor to the highest office in the land.

Hanson invokes the goddess Nemesis: She first makes mad those she intends to destroy. America's Media are mad. They are cuckoo. Certifiably insane. Nuts.

They are destroying their own businesses and the very country within which they operate, and they don't care.

We, the viewing public, have a front row seat. Talk about a reality show. We watch it on the screen every day. TV pundits no longer hide their lies as they rely upon the ignorance of you the viewer.

Yes, they think you are flat-out stupid and will believe anything they say and will act according to their wishes. But, uh-oh, the vast majority of the public isn't quite as credulous as Crunk News Network believed. What do they do? They threaten to destroy any who disagree with them. (See previous story as one example.)

What is that law in physics? That for every action there is an equal and opposite reaction?

Citizen Journalists are that equal and opposing reaction to the insanity that is the Socialist P.C. Media which, by the way, is as racist and prejudiced as the KKK and neo-Nazis. The harder the MSM tries to screw us over, the damn harder we're going to push back.

Informally stated: Don't poke me with that finger. Formally stated, Citizen Journalists' push-back is described by Newton's Third Law of Motion: "For every action, there is an equal and opposite reaction."

Forces always occur in pairs; when one body pushes against another, the second body pushes back just as hard. The statement means that in every interaction there is force acting on the two interacting objects. The size of the force on the first object equals the size of the force on the second.

MSM's actions in this matter clearly show they do not believe in science. Take a look here at Huffington Post's article calling for the execution of Trump:

Jason Fuller, Contributor
Working to bring about the best in America, both on line and off.

Impeachment Is No Longer Enough; Trump Must Face Justice

06/19/2017 10:39 pm ET

Impeachment and removal from office are only the first steps; for America to be redeemed, Donald Trump must be prosecuted for treason and—if convicted in a court of law—executed.

Dancing at the Waffle House

Draining the swamp means not only ejecting Trump from the presidency, but also bringing himself and **everyone** assisting in his agenda up on charges of treason. They must be convicted (there is little room to doubt their guilt). And then—upon receiving guilty verdicts—**they must all be executed under the law.** Anything less than capital punishment—or at least life imprisonment without parole in a maximum security detention facility—would send yet another message to the world that America has lost its moral compass. In order for America's morality and leadership to be restored, it must rebuke Donald Trump, his entire administration, and his legislative agenda in the strongest manner possible. And nothing would do more than to convict them of the highest offense defined by our Constitution, and then to deliver the ultimate punishment. Donald Trump deserves nothing less. Mitch McConnell, Steve Bannon, and Paul Ryan should also share Donald Trump's fate, for they have done more than practically anyone to protect him and to throw our country under the proverbial bus. In order to survive, we as a nation must deliver the ultimate punishment under the law to all involved in its current destruction.

Dancing at the Waffle House

Did HuffPo pull this particular article because it was a step too far, or because it was a step too quick?

Having jiggered their own poll in December 2016 to make it prove the point they wanted to prove, HuffPo has not backed off any anti-Trump sentiment. Which is why Jason Fuller's article was happily ensconced on their site with never a moment's hesitation.

But then the attack at the congressional baseball practice happened, and somebody noticed the article calling for Trump's execution because, as the article pointed out, "there is little room to doubt [his] guilt."

Oopsey.

Like a poker player showing his hand before the bets have been laid, HuffPo realized they were showing their extreme bias *before they should* and pulled the article.

But hey, somebody found a cached version of it on Google. Wanna see? I've included screen snips from the cache on previous pages. In any case, HuffPo still works as one of the anointed organs of Progressives/Socialists.

Now, what about the guy who wrote the article, Jason Fuller? Who is the guy? He says he's a regular dude working a low-paying job somewhere in flyover country. He says he really, really, really cares about assaults on civil liberties. He believes those assaults come from Trump and once a court signs off on his guilt, why we can simply get busy with the task at hand. And what is that task?

Why, executing Trump, of course.

Jason, Jason, Jason.

Bless your little old heart.

It's tough wanting to be a dictator but nobody will let you.

Page 74: Cached image on Google from article HuffPo pulled.

Page 75: Cached image on Google of a paragraph from the article that HuffPo pulled. *Underlining added by author.*

Dancing at the Waffle House

Eclipse Sales Pitch: Wham! Bam! Thank you, Ma'am! Or Why #CrunkNewsNetwork is still in business.

Dancing at the Waffle House

My friend R—, like most men, will use every opportunity to "gitsum" iffen yaknow whuttamean. Like soldiers going off to war have for all time been able to "gitsum" by using the threat of imminent death which includes them not returning alive, my friend R— used the last full solar eclipse to get inside the panties of some ladies.

That is, he sent out the offer. I have helpfully included a screenshot. Notice the second respondent below who "kinda don't wanna be alone for [the eclipse]" which, to my mind at least, means she's all for R— sharing some sausage. But otherwise, the sentiment was crude, quick, and pretty much was made fun of by the other respondents, of which I was one.

I replied to R—:
You forgot the lead up to it. Man, it's clear you are not in sales. Okay...your sales pitch should've gone like this and been sent via private message, so you don't look like the horn-dog that the above message made it seem you are. (Please notice I said "seem you are" which is called a CYA/Lawsuit-Avoiding weasel phrase as it does not come right out and say "you definitely are" a horn-dog.) Here is your script of what you should say to a woman:

"Baby, it has been widely reported on CNN and other news outlets that do NOT have fake news and who can be completely relied upon to keep us all

Dancing at the Waffle House

accurately up to date on anything that will affect our lives with a negative effect, that the world is ending as soon as the eclipse is over and that most, if not all, people will die. I would like my last thoughts to be of you before the big death is thrust upon us."

See, R—? You'll get better responses.

It didn't take long for R— to message me that his post was all in fun. I messaged back that I knew it was, and asked if he didn't get the humor in my reply. He replied, and I'm not kidding you, direct quote from R—:

I didn't read all through much to long

I'm not even going to mention the implications to his ability to satisfy a woman in bed that his sentence implies. How can he give proper attention to detail when it is needed? Eight words. Misspelled. Punctuation lacking.

But I mean, really, guys, can you imagine if a woman said that to you? "Well, you know, it's much too long." Would you like it, huh? I don't think so.

Size matters.

That is why R— is not a salesman in these matters. I'm sure R— will either unfriend me or agonize for days over that message because, unlike my dear readers, he does not yet understand long-form humor.

I bet he also honks exactly 0.0001 of a second after the light turns green.

Oh, R—, R— R—!

The ladies had such high expectations from you and you done dashed them to the ground and trampled on them.

R— has yet to respond to my obviously humorous and not bitter in the least private message implying that women don't like to be left hanging:

And that, R—, is why society believes misleading headlines. Jesus Christ and God Almighty. And let me tell you this, just so you know: If a man can't last for two short paragraphs, then I despair of his ability in bed.

The Psychosis of The Politically Correct

Psychosis: Abnormal condition of the mind involving a loss of contact with reality. Those experiencing psychosis present with personality changes including inability to think strategically or logically.

To be **politically correct** means never to speak up against the actions, thoughts, principles, and rules that are approved by dictators, and to eventually take on those dictators' standards as your own guiding lights.

Dancing at the Waffle House

United Network Command for Law and Enforcement.

Did you know the credits at the end of "The Man from U.N.C.L.E." state: We wish to thank the United Network Command for Law and Enforcement for their assistance?

That means they thank themselves. That's awesome. Ain't bragging if it's fact.

I especially liked the yellow triangle badges with employee numbers on them. Mr. Waverly, their boss, was 1. Iliya was 2 and Solo was 11. Never saw an UNCLE badge with more than two numbers. Of course, THRUSH badges (yes, with a bird) had numbers that went into three digits. One particularly lovely and efficient THRUSH agent was 897. She wore glasses and operated the computer.

The badge numbering makes it obvious that **UNCLE was Libertarian** because they believed in small government and nimble gitterdun attitudes that actually solved real problems.

Whereas **THRUSH** (The Technological Hierarchy for the Removal of Undesirables and the Subjugation of Humanity) **was obviously Progressive (Democrat and/or RINO)** as their staff was bloated; everybody did as they were told, no creative thinking at all. And to make a decision, well, they had to run it through the computer first, then debate it, then give speeches about why THRUSH would take over the world and UNCLE *would die. Muhwahahaha.*

THRUSH agents threw awesomely evil looks at UNCLE agents. When they looked at their compatriots, the added happy glint of evil plans coming to fruition simply made those glances even better. If looks could kill, THRUSH would've won every battle. Sort of like those pussy-hat-wearing celebrities and their mindless followers believe.

Today, UNCLE would love **#standfirm** and **#persevere** for that is what their expressions invoked. For them, resistance was not a state of being, it was a result of fighting evil, protecting the weak, defending the Constitution.

THRUSH would view such hashtags as a call to make more inner-city ghettos, set bad guys up in business, and gut and replace the Constitution while getting their hands on the money earned by citizens so they themselves could live in secure facilities and send their children to private schools under armed guard.

Oh, Solo and Iliya. We so need you now.

Dancing at the Waffle House

Socialist public schools punish victims, reward bullies.

My daughter called me. Seems her son, a fifth-grader, was attacked by a boy in his class. The boy had been doing stuff all year to my grandson. My grandson — a lot like his father, uncle, grandmother, great grandfather, and great-great grandfather — is a lover, not a fighter.

That is, he comes from a long line of peace-loving people who go out of their way to avoid conflicts chuckleheads like to chase.

But at the end of this school year the chucklehead in question was not to be avoided any longer. First, he hit my grandson, then opened a pair of scissors and threw them forcefully at him.

And that, according to my grandson in a statement most definitive, is when "I pounded on him and I won."

My grand got two days of in-school suspension. The principal said it was because he was fighting.

I don't like that. But I hear about and read stories like this all the time. In public schools the victims who defend themselves get punished most.

That is wrong. I will repeat: *That is wrong.*

My grandson's parents didn't agree with his punishment either, but neither spoke up. They each told him privately he did the right thing, but then they weren't in his corner against bad policy. Frankly, I couldn't believe it and told my daughter so.

"Nothing we can do about it," said she.

They don't see the end result of this inaction on their part. They supported the bully over the victim, whether they think so or not. They supported a Socialist principal against an innocent victim. They seem to think peace at all costs is the way to go.

But the long line mentioned above that my grand comes from know better. Each of us have made a habit of allowing chuckleheads every opportunity to walk away, but when the attack comes, we do not run, we respond definitively. Chucklehead does not come back.

As my grandson said, "He could've killed me with those scissors, so I had to hurt him."

Damn straight, boy.

And therein lies the problem.

"Bernie Sanders Rips Into Trump Budget Nominee For Past Christian Writings." This is the title of a YouTube video of a budget committee hearing. If you want to watch it, search YouTube using that title.

After watching it, the video is clear:

Lovable, cute, and cuddly Bernie the Socialist lets his true colors show. In this very public forum, he shows himself not to be so lovable, cute, and cuddly to Christian belief. His attack is typical of anyone who doesn't like it when the one attacked doesn't roll over, beg forgiveness, and ask to pretty please have his tummy tickled.

That is, when defense is clearly stated and stated again, Bernie interrupts his victim with "We don't have much time" and then promptly asks another question meant solely to inflame passions of any fellow Socialist who might be watching.

Well, he's got to earn those votes somehow. Hey, Vermont, did you see your boy in action here? Are you proud?

Dancing at the Waffle House

Writing on this unconstitutional action of Bernie "Feel the Bern" Sanders, David French said in the National Review, "Bernie Sanders would do well to brush up on his civic education and remember that religious freedom belongs even to citizens (and nominees) he doesn't like."

Of course, if the nominee were any other religion — I don't care which one, you name it as long as it is not Christian — Bernie would have been all grins and giggles, slobbering on himself in his haste to get that most awesome and perfectly suited nominee confirmed.

And why would that be? Because Bernie cares deeply, so very, very deeply? Not really. He doesn't care for anything but his own secret agenda, which is that he wants to rule the world. As any good Socialist wants to.

And therein lies the problem.

See Something, Say Something.

Labor Day weekend 2017 found me in beautiful Downtown Decatur, Georgia, where the AJC Decatur Book Festival was being held for the twelfth year.

I am part of a group of female crime novelists (Sisters in Crime — Atlanta Chapter) who rented tent space. Other than a mere mention in official festival literature of where our tent was, you wouldn't know that we had two days of panelists featuring twenty-four authors who write a wide range of crime fiction. From cozies to thrillers, we cover it. Why we were not in the official listing of things to see and do is another story for another time.

But as an exhibitor, I received a packet containing letters from the mayor and festival president as well as instructions on how to collect, report, and turn in sales tax.

But these weren't the best things in the packet. The best was a notice entitled:

"See Something, Say Something."

You need to understand that Decatur, Georgia, is where the Politically Correct hang out. We have Emory University and Agnes Scott College, the CDC, a VA hospital, and several coffee shops run by men in exquisitely coiffed long beards and man buns, matching suspenders and flannel shirts, and sporting skinny-leg skintight jeans that make a female wonder where he keeps his junk, you know, like his wallet and keys.

In other words, in this city one does not make public that one has a concealed carry permit if one wants to have anybody to talk to. Verboten subjects: Guns, guns, and guns.

These kind folks are accepting of people from everywhere. The City of Decatur attracts the best and the brightest from around the world and is a hotbed of creativity from medicine, science, and technology to art, literature, and music.

That's why I found it interesting and not a little bit unnerving that exhibitors were given these instructions.

"If you see something suspicious taking place, or see a suspicious package, then report that behavior or activity to [contact info was inserted here]."

All that was fine and made sense. The next paragraph is the kicker as it had to define what is ***not to be*** considered suspicious:

"Factors such as race, ethnicity, national origin, or religious affiliation alone are not suspicious. For that reason, the public should report only suspicious behavior and situations (e.g., an unattended backpack in a public place or someone trying to break into a restricted area) ***rather than beliefs, thoughts, ideas, expressions, associations, or speech unrelated to terrorism or other criminal activity.***"

That the festival organizers thought so little of their exhibitors that they felt the need to remind them to be tolerant was insulting in the extreme. Yet if any exhibitor had seen something and said something, they would've been called racist, prejudiced, and some-sort-of-ism-phobic, and barred from future exhibiting.

You think I'm wrong?

Just ask the government employees who designed Thinthread, or Philip Haney, a founding member of the Department of Homeland Security, or FBI agents coming forward with proof of dirty deeds done by their bosses. All were threatened with legal action and hounded out of service for seeing something and saying something.

Dancing at the Waffle House

Cowboys and Indians and Posers.

Which is worse?

One: Using Granny's comments that high cheekbones on an ancestor proved he was a Native American Indian, then claiming inclusion in that minority class, and therefore asserting the right to get the set-aside job?

Or, two: Being outraged for the dissing a minority class has taken because somebody is lying about their inclusion in their class in order to steal the honor (and jobs) from members of that minority class?

Dancing at the Waffle House

In the world of the Pussy-Hat Wearing Politically Correct Democrat Liberal RINO Socialist Fascist Commie, the second one is worse, with them going so far as to say that the very use of the name Pocahontas is a racial slur.

Earth to P-HWPCDLRSFCs!

Here is the actual quote where Donald Trump said the so-called slur:

"So that was the ultimate statement from General Kelly, the importance. And I want to thank you because you're very, very special people. **You were here long before any of us were here, although we have a representative in Congress who, they say, was here a long time ago. They call her 'Pocahontas.'**"

See? Trump was not insulting the Code Talkers or, for that matter, any Native American Indian. He was honoring their heritage by politely pointing out that others do not honor it and are willing to lie about their heritage, steal the thunder of another's heritage, and otherwise act like a poser.

In fact, the entire brouhaha the Mainstream Media and Pussy-Hat Wearing Politically Correct Democrat Liberal RINO Socialist Fascist Commie crowd ginned up has itself taken away from the Code Talkers being honored.

Dancing at the Waffle House

As far back as 2012, when it came to light that highly respected universities had hired Elizabeth Warren so they could *claim* they were meeting diversity quotas without actually having to sully their hallowed halls with yet another member of a needy minority class, Mark Steyn said —

"Alas, the actual original marriage license does not list Great-Great-Great-Gran'ma as Cherokee, but let's cut Elizabeth Fauxcahontas Crockagawea Warren some slack here. She couldn't be black. She would if she could, but she couldn't. But she could be 1/32nd Cherokee, and maybe get invited to a luncheon with others of her kind – 'people who are like I am,' **31/32nds white** – and they can all sit around celebrating their diversity together. She is a testament to America's melting pot, composite pot, composting pot, whatever."

Dancing at the Waffle House

Dancing at the Waffle House

You want I should go naked?

Dancing at the Waffle House

Through reasoned articles in highfalutin' publications, children's stories read to us by teachers, and movies acted out for us, we've been told for at least fifty years the benefits to all mankind of accepting different cultures.

Kumbaya fairly dripped out of fashion magazines as they showed one white person after another swapping clothing, trying new hairstyles, cooking different foods, adding different colors to their walls and paintings, trying new jewelry styles, and more — all inspired by what we now call The Cultures of Persons of Color.

Persons of Color did not mind this. They thought it was awesome. Indeed, the campaign for inclusiveness was wildly successful. I mean, look...I know more white people with dreads than I know blacks with them.

But the big question is: Why was the campaign for inclusiveness successful?

Simple: Because it was white people doing all the including — and they did a damn fine job of it, too.

Case in point of how much striving for excellence in inclusiveness white folks have done:

I was helping out a venue that was putting on a show that featured Native Africans, all except one who was black (he was a white

Dancing at the Waffle House

South African), playing and singing Native African music. Ninety-eight percent of the audience was white. Toward the end of the show, one band invited all the people to stand and feel the music with them.

Oh, lots of clapping and shoulder shaking and stamping in place was going on. Running from the back came a white woman who got right next to the stage and started doing a Native African dance better than they could. I know this because the band stared at her hard and looked at each other — then at me with shrugs of "Whut? Huh?" — as this woman pushed her bubble butt up higher than her head and bounced it around in a perfect imitation of a tribal dance.

So you see, the more white people took into their daily lives the fashions (and cultural dances) of non-whites, then non-whites themselves began wearing more of their cultures' fashions and adopting more of their cultures' dances.

Were they waiting on whites to give them permission to be who they really were? I don't know, but it is an interesting question, isn't it?

But as they all do, this Pendulum of Inclusiveness swung back and it swung back hard.

Dancing at the Waffle House

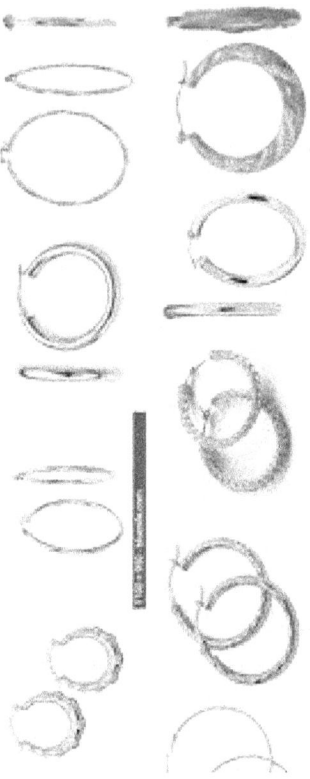

Hoops such as these have now been proclaimed as being for the exclusive use of People of Color.

Dancing at the Waffle House

That's right. People of Color are now saying that — let me quote a Woman of Color from Claremont College — "...our winged eyeliner, lined lips, and big hoop earrings [serve] as symbols [and] as an everyday act of resistance..."

And who has to change yet again? Of course! White people. After fifty years of training by the Caring Left, and a massive investment, all that has happened is now white people are evil if they wear hoop earrings.

They might want to tell these folks about that. Johnny Depp especially, since he wears hoops *and* winged eyeliner.

Google Search screenshots of famously liberal men who proudly support Brown power wearing hoop earrings.

Google Search screenshots of women who simply like hoop earrings because they are cool.

You want I should go naked?

Dancing at the Waffle House

Now we trade in the Old Politically Correct Inclusiveness for the New Politically Correct Exclusiveness. The very people who rail against being excluded are now themselves practicing exclusion with gusto.

Before too long, they're going to require all white folks go naked to prove they aren't appropriating anybody's culture. Then somebody's going to say, "Hey, wait. They are trying to be just like that Tribe of Brown Shade in That Country Over There" and a whole new campaign will start up. Can't win for damn losing.

The politics of boobs.

I have two children. I breastfed both…in public. I did not know I was a Breastfeeding Advocate. These days, the topic is hot. Even the friendly pope has weighed in on this. I chose to breastfeed for these reasons, in this order.

One: It was cheap. My body manufactured food and fed a human for several months. When I did the math comparing the cost of formula plus time to prepare and warm and fill bottles, against free and I could sleep while baby suckled? Hands-down, breastfeeding got my vote.

Two: It was good for the baby. Lifelong health benefits. I'm delivering antibodies and such as that with a mere suckle? Done.

But publicly flaunting the process? Never…except that one time in the van when her daddy and I were riding down the road and a truck driver kept "admiring the baby", who had unbeknownst to me unbuttoned my blouse and was flashing the guy on my behalf.

Oh, yeah. There was that other time in church when the same child unbuttoned another blouse of her mother, who was so intent on listening to the lesson and wondering why the guy on the stage kept looking at her that she didn't hear the sermonizing. God only knows how long that nursing bra was showing.

But other than those times, never once did I publicly flaunt the Feed-O-Mats. When I nursed, I kept a lightweight blankee over the process. Many times, people had no clue I was being a Breastfeeding Advocate because marching in the street is not my way.

So. Boobs.

Sexual healing or food delivery system?

Well, our Heavenly Father says both.

Seeing as how he designed the body and boobs to do the above for children, Proverbs 5:19 tells a husband to let his wife's boobs feed his soul this way: "Let her breasts satisfy you at all times; be exhilarated always with her love."

I don't think God was talking about a snack.

But, you wait and see if some feminazi, who claims she cares about all mankind, doesn't pop up and march in the street nursing her child demanding Congress do something about the repression of women. Oh, wait. That's already happening. Holy cow! There is a Facebook page, too. There was even a sit-in.

Sigh.

The politics of boobs. Judging from the number of pages the National Geographic devotes to naked women in third-world countries, they understand the importance of boobs to the developing psyches and political opinions of young boys in first-world countries.

And what about the rioting, gang-banging Muslims in Germany and India, among other countries, wilding in the streets, group groping and raping? Obviously, these — let me be polite — *fundamentalists* take issue with boobs, and turn them into political jihad against the Decadent West.

The Decadent West.

Got to love that term. When was the last time you saw or heard about thousands of men (of any color or religious persuasion) in the US and certain other EU countries roaming the streets en masse and attacking women?

It doesn't happen.

And I'll tell you why.

Because. Real. Men. Don't.

Real Men (and they are the majority) know their babies need good food and they are happy their wives are good mommies and they aren't jealous of their kiddies eating a good meal.

Once babies start on solid food and Mama gets some rest from those boobs being kept wet and chapped from leaking milk because baby slept longer than normal, and by sloppy little slurping mouths biting with sharp new little teeth using the nipple as a teething ring, and pinching with little hands and sharp fingernails as they try to get to din-din fast, then and only then do Real Men know that Mama gonna want some soul food of her own.

And Real Men…oh, yeah…they know what to do for Mama…and they aren't asking Congress for guidance or permission.

And me? I didn't ask permission to do what was best needed for my child. I just did it. Quietly. No grandstanding. No TV interviews.

Because that's what Real Women do.

Opinion, Varied

If you have previously self-identified as a member of the Pussy-Hat Wearing Politically Correct Democrat Liberal RINO Socialist Fascist Commie crowd, and you chose to read this book anyway, that you've gotten this far means I have two things to say to you:

Kudos, and welcome to the real world.

Dancing at the Waffle House

Dancing at the Waffle House.

My ex-husband used to say to me, "Angie." That's what he called me, Angie. "Angie," he'd say, "you can dance to an alarm clock."

He was right. I can. I was born with rhythm. Do not confuse what I just said with *I was conceived via the Rhythm Method.* That is not what I said. What I said was, my rhythm is DNA deep. I did not learn it. It is simply there.

So, when I hear music, or any rhythmic pattern say from a train on a track or whatever, my body naturally starts moving in time. Often, I'm not even aware I'm dancing. This rhythm of mine has gotten me in trouble, cranked up party fun, and caused people to laugh. Which brings us to the title of this article.

This morning I was having my Waffle House cheesy eggs (on the side, add onions and ham; no raisin toast or scattered and covered) when this fella put some money in the jukebox and up cranked this song: Cameo's *Word Up.*

I know, right? Isn't it just a totally freaking awesome song? Now, you got to understand that when I go out dancing and this song comes on, you better just not even think of holding on to me as I've got my own little choreographed movements to it. I've danced to it so often the movements just happen at the right time.

Okay. Here I am. Waffle House. Cheesy eggs. Reading a book. Sipping my coffee and WORD UP! WHOOT-WHOOT! And here goes my body, *do my dance, do my dance, do my dance for me* while sitting and still reading and sipping coffee.

I will not describe for you here the reactions of the other diners as you probably already know. My only wish is that nobody was filming it. But God help me if right after *Word Up!* ended James Brown came on funking it up all over the Waffle House with his *Get On Up.*

Dang.

Where's a man's belt buckle when you need one to shine?

Living life *tempo rubato*.

"Angela, what do you want to be when you grow up?"

I could never answer that question quickly enough, so I learned to make up an answer that would satisfy the teacher in front of me. The most popular answer was, "I want to be a teacher." They always smiled.

The thing is, I am a teacher. I live, learn, and pass it on. If you read *Twinkle, a memoir*, you'll understand more of what drove me and moved me and thus how I got to where I was at the time of the writing. But only with that clarity and the passing of time — that is, the clock pushing ever onward to inevitable death — does one have the length of years to study and learn about how the rest of one's life will look. What have I learned about me?

Dancing at the Waffle House

I've learned that I live *tempo rubato*.

Tempo rubato is Italian for stolen time. It is a musical term referring to expressive and rhythmic freedom by a slight speeding up and then slowing down of the tempo of a piece at the discretion of the soloist or conductor, and everybody else follows the pace. In other words, free in the presentation.

This does not mean I live my life willy-nilly, giving no thought to making plans or having no care for others. No way. A soloist or a conductor cannot indulge in *tempo rubato* if they do not know the score inside and out. Further, those they play with must know the score that well, too. But that is on the stage.

Living *tempo rubato* off-stage is apt to be influenced by unknown unknowns. Living *tempo rubato* in the real world is difficult.

Yet, here I am doing it. Living *tempo rubato* is not the path to riches. It isn't even the path to financial stability. (Rich men typically don't want a woman like myself. Unthinking arm candy I am not and can't subjugate my life to such; there goes that form of income.) And while money is "for a protection", I find it easier to live like Apostle Paul who was content in whatever financial condition he found himself. Paul knew, as do I, that financial stability is not the most important thing in life.

Nor is it the most important thing to God. Having studied my life, I came to realize that God has been in control the whole time. He has pushed me where He needed me to be *whether or not I understood it, and even if it made me despair.* And somehow it always works out fine though, frankly, my ego takes a beating as oftentimes my personal desires and plans don't work out.

People are always saying to me, "Angela, you are so smart and talented. What are *you* doing *here?*" My answer? Living *tempo rubato* is where God has put me, that's why. Yes, I have a deep grasp of life and people and business and issues and more that could make me a lot of money. And yes, I would love to make more money and not have to worry as much about the future.

I want things settled, damn it, because living with unknown unknowns is hard work.

Dancing at the Waffle House

But every time opportunities I like peek their heads above the horizon, they are smacked down like so many whack-a-moles at Chuck E. Cheese, and I am pushed, shoved in another direction.

That direction, by the by, always works out for the greater good of something or someone,

but maybe not always for me. Yes, I complain about that, but not living *tempo rubato* is impossible for me because this is how God has made me. This is where He wants me.

The many things I have been pushed into that, on my own, I would never have thought to do. The many people I have met that

Dancing at the Waffle House

I did not know existed. Only living *tempo rubato* has given me these and fed my soul.

Not a bad way to live at all. And now that I've learned not to fight it, better unknown unknowns happen even faster.

Mr. Romance is the best boyfriend ever. Linda Sands, my good friend and fellow crime novelist, introduced us a few years ago. Mr. Romance believes in supporting his woman, so he came out to see one of my live shows, a house concert I did with pianist extraordinaire Alan Dynin.

HELP IMPROVE YOUR HEALTH: BUY SOMETHING FROM ME!

9 out of 10 doctors recommend humor to improve health.*

*One doctor out of 10 is always a sour puss.

If I self-identify as a Female Native American Caribbean-African Disabled Male Machinist HB1/2 Righty-Tighty-Lefty-Loosey Author, will my books sell faster?

Book Marketing 101: If you want to sell books, you've got to have a platform. Sometimes building that platform involves murder. But, if you don't want to kill somebody, then you must find another way to get that platform upon which marketing campaigns are built.

Here are the problems with my marketing platform. I am not, am no longer, or have never:

1. Been 20 years old and —
2. Posed nude (except when I was three weeks old, but that doesn't count)
3. Taken nude pictures of others (don't ask what I've taken of myself)

4. Robbed a bank and used the money to pay for cancer treatments
5. Been an atheist that...what *do* they do?
6. Killed anybody or covered up a crime
7. Been a meth/pot/crack head who came back and founded a multimillion-dollar empire
8. Married a gangster or other public personality
9. Divorced a gangster or other public personality
10. Had an affair with a married gangster or other public personality or their spouse
11. Had my life threatened by a gangster or other public personality or their spouse
12. Lived out of my car and then gone on to set up a multibillion-dollar empire

The list could go on, but you get the gist. I simply blend in with all the other law-abiding folks who calmly and quietly go about their lives.

However, I've come up with a marketing plan. Let me know if you think it will work.

If I self-identify as a Female Native American Caribbean-African Disabled Male HB1/2 Machinist Righty-Tighty-Lefty-Loosey Author, will my books sell faster?

More importantly, will agents and publishers compete over my unpublished manuscripts with exclamations of "Wow! Does she ever have a great platform! Let's sign her because that's less work we have to do and less money we have to put out. Profit!" (Three exclamation points on purpose because that is how much enthusiasm they will have for me and my book.)

You think I jest? I am quite serious, and I thank you for giving me your opinion on this matter. Here is a list of recent stories, in the headlines mind you. I can't make this stuff up. Lots of other people are doing outrageous things as they self-identify.

OMGee! Look at all the *free column inches* these people get in newspapers. That's money straight to the bottom line if they're selling something.

- Man marries computer in New Mexico. Alabama does not recognize the marriage. Man sues.
- White woman, Rachel Dolezal, self-identifies as black, and will not apologize or stop doing it.
- All-female Spelman College will admit men who self-identify as women.

- To get a teaching job, Elizabeth Warren claims to be part Native American.
- Toronto's Ryerson University made a policy change to create a more inclusionary environment for students. That's right. You don't have to self-identify as anything. In fact, they'd rather you not.
- To get greater diversity on the provincial bench, Ontario is making changes to its judicial applications: Please, oh, please, self-identify as something we can count, even disabled.
- And Regnery, the nation's premier publisher of conservative books, will no longer allow authors to self-identify with the New York Times best-seller list seeing as how the NYT is such a manipulator and very left-leaning anyway.

Whoa. Now that's an idea I could steal: Self-identify as a BEST SELLER from the git-go.

You Know the Tune: If I Had a Hammer
(The Terrorist Version)

If I had a hammer
>I'd hammer on your head
>I'd hammer till it's red
>All over this land
>I'd hammer out your brains
>I'd hammer out your eyes
>I'd hammer out hate between
>My brothers and infidels
>All over this land, uh, uh

If I could send you to hell
>I'd send you in the morning
>I'd send you in the evening
>All over this land
>I'd signal I'm danger
>I'd signal out a warning
>I'd signal out hate between
>My brothers and infidels
>All over this land, oh.

Dancing at the Waffle House

If I had a bomb
    I'd blow it in the morning
    I'd blow it in the evening
    All over this land
    I'd blow up your children
    I'd blow up your trannies
    I'd blow up hate between
    My brothers and infidels
    All over this land, oh
Well, I've got a hammer
    And I'll send you to hell
    And I've got a bomb to blow
    All over this land
It's the hammer of jihad
    It's the hell of slavery
    It's the bomb of hate between
    My brothers and infidels
    All over this land
It's the hammer of jihad
    It's the hell of slavery
    It's the bomb of hate between
    My brothers and infidels
    All over this land

    With sincere apologies to songwriters Lee Hays and Pete Seeger. *If I Had a Hammer* lyrics © T.R.O. Inc.
    Parody Lyrics Angela K. Durden © 2017

Networked Fourth Estate: Citizen Journalists Carry the Torch.

The Patriot Act, mass surveillance, and all that other nasty stuff coming to light these days exists because people, citizens, allowed government too much control. How does government get that kind of control? The same way an elephant is eaten: One small bite at a time.

Hitler did not rise to power overnight. He had a plan. He showed he cared for the German people. He created jobs. Heck, he ordered the design of a mass-produced car called the Volkswagen Beetle that everybody could ride on the brand spanking new country-wide highway system he was building.

Wasn't Hitler simply ever so nice? He cares about us, the German people decided. Jobs. Cars. New roads. Of course, what he wasn't telling the populace was that these super-stout highways were for the sole purpose of quickly moving heavy war machines and soldiers from one place to another. And they thought it was for making their vacay trip easy. But…

Surprise! World War Two.

Dancing at the Waffle House

And if you complain, O Citizenry, we shall kill you. Your children are ours. Also ours? Your businesses and lives. Yes, Hitler and his gang decided to rule the world according to their enlightened ways, which were nothing but intolerant, narrow-minded, conformist in the extreme, partial to themselves, and decidedly unenlightened.

Hitler ended up killing himself. Yay.

In the United States those bites against civil liberties and basic human rights started in earnest in the '60s when a concerted and concentrated effort began to gut the very foundations of this country, namely the Constitution and the Bill of Rights. Madalyn Murray O'Hair was a huge front-runner of it with her assault on getting rid of all prayer in schools, though, truthfully, she simply saw how the wind was blowing and took advantage of it to make a name for herself.

In any case...

This gutting of the Constitution and the Bill of Rights didn't happen overnight, and it continues today. You want to know why so much anti-Trump stuff is in the news? Because by daring to say he would protect and defend the Constitution and the Bill of Rights, President Trump is threatening to overturn all efforts of those who have worked hard to turn government that *serves* into a "Nanny State", a big government that controls by convincing each succeeding generation they are too stupid to make simple choices about their lives.

Oh, how they are investing millions if not billions in pushing their agenda of hate.

They loved Trump the mogul and reality TV star. They hate the Trump that defends against their tyranny.

They love the tax-paying conservative citizenry that provides them their spending money. They hate the "basket of deplorables" — a much larger crowd than their wildest dreams ever expected — that agree with defending the Constitution and protecting the Bill of Rights.

Dripping Hate

All this hate drips from newspaper headlines, magazine covers, and serious news shows on major networks owned and controlled by the so-called enlightened but whose circulation, subscriptions, and ratings have been falling for years and they cannot figure out why.

"See, we know best!" they and their handmaidens still crow. "You (viewer, reader, and citizen) are a mere idiot and cannot hope to understand. WE will teach your children what is best. WE will tell you when you can move. WE are the enlightened. You want to know how stupid you are, parents? WE, the progressives, will say it: You are too stupid to even tell your children how babies are made or how to avoid pregnancy."

State-Sponsored Censuring

So, the State provides teachers trained in State-approved methods to teach children in State-sponsored schools who are given State-approved materials and measured against State-approved tests designed to keep citizens in their places.

The State punishes parents who dare question what their children are taught. The State upbraids and censures parents who dare to teach their children that the best way, the very best way, to avoid getting pregnant is to use self-control and not have sex until such time as they are ready to support a child.

"What?" says the State, shocked at the impudence of such parents. "Self-control? Your children cannot exercise self-control because they are animals, living in their reptilian brain, and when they feel an urge — whether it to be creative and sing, or boink willy-nilly the gender of their choice — They. Must. Not. Be. Hindered. Else their precious egos take a beating and they won't be able to reach their full potential. Oh, the horror."

Take Hope

But it is those of us like myself who also write, who are part of a strong networked fourth estate of Citizen Journalists indebted to none, bound to truth, upholders of justice for all who know we carry weight and are making a difference because social media titans block us, ban us, shut down our accounts, or in other ways make sure nobody sees our clear messages of what the real problem is:

The fight to take away freedom.

For those who read these writings, for those who share the messages they read, for those who take heart from them all, we are working our fingers as fast as we can.

Dancing at the Waffle House

The New War on Women is a War on Real Men: The New PC Power Grab.

The War Between the Sexes has existed since Adam and Eve. Though this war has been fought since forever, it has always been fought so that peace will reign between Mars and Venus. This war is not what this article is about.

This article is about the terrorists among us who have started a new war on females that is, in truth, a war on real men.

Weapon of choice: Attack the men through their women.

Transgender men are not new, and many families handle the situation perfectly fine. For eons every generation, religion, socio-economic class, and country has had their share, though India seems to have more than their fair share, even having whole communities with a well-defined subculture and gurus. But even that is not what this article is about.

Don't be mistaken in thinking that the newest permutation of the war on females is brand spanking new. The reason this new war has gotten as far as it has these days is because it wears new clothes.

Yes, Fake Transgender Males Who Pretend to Want to be Women have changed their dresses and used the power of Political Correctness to deploy the Force of Law to attack men by attacking what they care about most:

Their daughters, wives, mothers, sisters, aunties, cousins, and grandmothers.

There has never been not one transgender person who has ever had a problem finding a bathroom. Ever. Never ever.

That is the truth.

Truth does not matter to terrorists.

What matters to them is power, and they don't care what lie they have to tell or who they have to manipulate to get it. They'll say it and they'll do it — even if it means reaching into the highest office of the land for a dupe.

When the sitting president of the United States pushed the transgender agenda down the throats of its citizens without asking them what they thought — that is, without debate and by decree, like a dictator — that is when real men said enough.

Thank goodness we got a real man to rescind those federal guidelines and let individual communities make up their own minds about how they want to handle it.

Both Trump and the men who fought against the Bathroom Dictate were demonized by the Mainstream Media. Leading that charge was that venerable handmaiden of terror itself, the Crunk News Network.

But these fake transgender men aren't the only ones who hate men.

Socialists, every member of ISIS, and most practitioners of Fundamental [insert any religion here] who say they hate women with a fierce passion hate men worse. They control men by holding hostage their females.

One crucial thing you have to understand is that these individuals and groups will come after any man who stands up for women. Here's why —

These are tried-and-true methods of war.

Invading armies rape women. Raping accomplishes three things.

One: It leaves behind children with the DNA of the invading army.

Two: It demoralizes the men.

Three: Seeing their women hurt, the men get so mad they can't think straight, making them easier to subdue.

The Obama decree was seen for what it was. Not as protections for those who truly are what God made them, but as legal protection for sexual predators who get their jollies from threatening women in order to metaphorically cuckold other men.

Puddles, Negan, DragonCon, and my failure to serve you well as Citizen Journalist.

Not to be confused with Puddles Pita Party, which involves some sort of lap dog with a bladder problem eating hummus and olives, Atlanta's own Puddles Pity Party is now known to the entire population of the US who watches "America's Got Talent."

I do not watch "America's Got Talent", but I do know people behind Puddles' success, and I think I met him once when he was incognito as himself. But I'm not bragging.

This article is not about the original seven-foot-tall white male in whiteface, Puddles The Clown, or his Pity Party. It is about me going to DragonCon and not being the Citizen Journalist I promised I would be for you, Dear Readers.

You see, I went to DragonCon Atlanta on Labor Day Weekend 2017 because my good friend and fellow crime novelist Linda Sands dragged me. "We're gonna see some weird shit," she promised.

It is obvious Linda has no clue what I grew up around, so frankly, I was somewhat bored though there was this one fella...yeah...he was right handsome, and I got a hug-and-a-pic with him. Back to my apology about falling down on my job as Citizen Journalist.

While mostly I was walking around and taking pictures and trying my very best to get into the spirit of the thing, there came a point where I was tired of holding my phone and put it in my purse.

Shame. On. Me.

Of all people, I should know that the best stories are not made, they simply often walk by just begging to be told. Such a story happened at DragonCon but because I was too slow I missed it. Let me assure faithful readers that two wines, one champagne, and one rather generous White Russian had absolutely nothing to do with my lapse. Here's what I missed documenting in a photo.

Puddles the Clown showed up in whiteface, but this Puddles was a black man in whiteface. I hesitate to say the man was African-American as I did not hear his voice nor was I able to interview him to ask his heritage. Anybody reading this who takes offense at me mentioning the black man in whiteface needs to realize I am doing my best not to offend his racial heritage by calling him something he isn't.

See, this guy could be visiting from South Africa, where he is a citizen. To call him an African-American South African is both journalistically and factually incorrect.

Furthermore, I believe he was from way out of town because no African-American in their right mind from the US would ever insult white folks by showing up in whiteface and pretending to be a white male, right?

That won't happen, will it?

DragonCon Puddles did a fine job of looking serious and somewhat put out, that is, staying in character. In fact, when I saw him — I swear I ain't lying — he looked right in my eyes and simply dared me to come say something to him so he could not speak to me.

Why oh why did I not jump all over that opportunity? I am so sorry you won't be able to read the silent interview.

Dancing at the Waffle House

The smaller the stakes, the fiercer the fight.

Bookending two recent weekends was a writer/publisher/agent convention called Killer Nashville, which I attended for the first time and wherein I had one fine blast and installed and began to use this new app for my iPhone called Snapchat.

The other was the twelfth annual AJC Decatur Book Festival, wherein the main reason I had fun was because I was with my fellow Atlanta chapter Sisters in Crime in a tent we shared with the Southeast chapter of Mystery Writers of America.

From cozy mysteries where the crimes happen off the page to thrillers where the good guys kidnap the bad guys and use mind games to make them write their confessions to fun and snarky rock'em-sock'em action, we Sisters (and a couple of Misters) know how to kill you and get rid of the body while at the same time solving the crime.

But this article is not about those fine authors or organizations.

Dancing at the Waffle House

Sayre's law states: In any dispute the intensity of feeling is inversely proportional to the value of the issues at stake.

To that I add: That is why the book publishing business is so viciously petty.

At Killer Nashville, I signed up for a pitch session that was scheduled the hour before I was to moderate a bevy of kick-ass panelists, only one of whom I had ever met. Explaining my situation, the two agents allowed me to pitch first and leave the room since I had to get things set up and make sure all was well. The next day, I saw one of the agents. Now, I've been good and properly dissed in my lifetime, so I know dissing when I see it. I was dissed with the best eye roll you ever saw accompanied by a click of the tongue on her teeth.
I laughed.

Turning the page to next weekend...

Taking my turn handing out brochures to passersby at the AJC Decatur Book Festival, I was smiling and engaging with book lovers of all sorts. I talked to old and young, white and black, Asian and undetermined. (It was the same weekend as DragonCon, after all.)

Then I saw this couple walking toward me. I can only describe them as smooth. That is, their clothes were crisply starched and ironed. Their hair was perfection itself. Even their skin looked like it had no imperfections. I doubt either had ever broken a sweat in their lives. Both the man and woman seemed to be somewhere between 45 and 60 years old; these days it's hard to tell ages.

But hey, they looked like they could afford books. I myself, an author of over fifteen books, several of novel length, was taking my turn handing out marketing materials for our booth. So I approached this couple and said in quite a friendly fashion —

"Hello. Are you fans of murder, mystery, and mayhem?"

At this I point to the sign showing that branding slogan along with the logos of the two groups whose authors are represented.

Remember I told you that I've been dissed good and proper before, so I know when I'm being dissed. I got dissed again by this smooth couple.

First, they stopped dead in their tracks.

Second, their noses locked onto me like laser beams. Those noses quickly traced a pattern from my head to toes and back again.

Third, the woman rolled her eyes, and looked away with such an elegant snort of derision that I was impressed.

Fourth, as if I had missed the big sign above their heads announcing it, and I'm not kidding you, he said, "We're authors."

"We're authors."

"We're authors."

We. Are. Authors.

Hahahaha. I can't say that enough.

I wanted to holler after them, "Oh, yeah? But are you selling any books?"

Because frankly, if you've got to advertise the fact in such a petty fashion, then it's a sure bet you aren't selling any. Further, it's a sure bet you can't figure out why you are successful in your other life but can't sell a damn book.

At Killer Nashville, I asked a question of the agent mentioned above. I said, "How difficult is it to sell a publisher on a book?"

Her first unguarded reaction told me all I needed to know. She isn't selling many at all. You need to understand that she's only been in the publishing game for a year. Being an agent looks fun and sexy, but if you do it right, it is damn hard work. Like many, she thought she would only have to snap her fingers and become the next kingmaker.

After all, how hard is it to form an opinion on what makes a book the public will like? Like many who have such an opinion, she thought she had the agent's role all figured out. I know this because her introduction to the pitch group was: **"I look for books I can fix."**

Oh, honey. It's a good thing you have a rich husband in Big Pharma. You must have a lot of free time on your hands.

Her idea of "fixing" my book — based on reading two double-spaced pages — was that on the first page I had to include gory details of the torture murder and make the woman who found the evidence the main protagonist.

On the first page.

No wonder she's not selling anything.

Dancing at the Waffle House

Angela answers job interview questions from hell.

Job interview questions from hell deserve the answers they get. I've never had an easy time finding jobs that match my abilities. There are very good reasons for that, explaining why I

was able to make more money by starting my own business. When applying for jobs, questions I get asked never draw answers expected by interviewers. They don't know what to do with my answers.

But here, for your amusement, are my answers to those job interview questions from hell recently reported on by that friendly megalithic employer called MSN.

Dancing at the Waffle House

I advise the reader to categorically understand that I do not lie.

That is, in my novels I make up stories, and in my satirical and humorous columns the truth is obviously stretched to make a point, but when it comes to me, no lying. Granted, the whole truth is not always told. When you read below you will understand why.

But I do not lie.

That is, I do not make up out of whole cloth nor stretch the truth when I talk about myself. If anything, I often hold back. And do that so often that when somebody eventually finds out more about me they invariably say, "Oh. My. GOD! Angela, I had no idea you did [fill in a thing here]. You are so…so…[fill in flattering descriptor here but which usually ends up sounding like You Are The Most Brilliant Woman In The World.]"

I kid you not. It's embarrassing. Granted, my ego likes it, but it becomes humiliating because other questions usually follow and it's the answers to those that are harder for people to process. Read on. You'll see why Angela has always had a difficult time getting a job.

1. "What on your CV is the closest thing to a lie?"

Angela's Answer: You calling me a *liar*?

2. "What am I thinking right now?"
   Angela's Answer: *[Sigh]* I'm...not looking for a boyfriend.

3. "If you had a friend who was great for a job and an identical person who was just as good, but your friend earned your company $2,000 less, who would you give the job to?"
   Angela's Answer: The other person. Duh. However, the premise of the question has nothing to do with reality. For instance, *how* do I know the other person could, in point of fact, earn my company more than my friend? Am I not interviewing both? And since we know that past performance does not guarantee future results, the question is just silly. I need more information.

4. "What's the most selfish thing you've ever done?"
   Angela's Answer: Well, there was that one time I ate the sugar cubes I was supposed to give the horses. But I was hungry. And I was six.

5. "You are stranded on the moon with a group of other astronauts and you need to travel 200 miles back to base. Here is a list of 15 items

salvaged from the wreckage of the spacecraft you were traveling in. List them in order of importance."

Angela's Answer: [Reading over the list.] Why would anyone take these things to the moon? What idiot thought these things would help in any way in outer space? Whoever made this list has never been to the moon. They did not ask for advice about what conditions are like there. And furthermore, there's a base on the moon? Don't they have walkie-talkies and such as that? And if they don't, then what kind of planning went into this project anyway? And if they crashed, why are they 200 miles away? Did they think they'd find a Home Depot or Ace Hardware?

6. "How would you describe cloud computing to a seven-year-old?"

Angela's Answer: What does this kid already know? What is their frame of reference? I mean, is this a genius kid or a regular kid or what? What country does this kid live in? I would have to ask lots of questions of the kid to determine what they know in order to explain it to him. Otherwise I'd just be bumping my gums, you know?

7. "There are three people, each with different salaries, and they want to find the average of them without telling any of the other two their salary. How do they do it?"

Angela's Answer: Who is "they" that wants to find out? Can't "they" ask each of the three privately and do computations in their own office?

8. "You have 50 red and 50 blue objects. Split these however you like between two containers to give the minimum/maximum probability of drawing one of the colors."

Angela's Answer: Sure. Okay. The question I would ask, however, is this: If I tell you, can you prove I'm wrong? And if you say yes, then I have to ask on what basis can you prove that? And if you say you were told the result should be a certain thing, then of course I have to completely suspect the validity of this question and your ability to hire. If you have not independently confirmed the answer from a minimum of two sources who agree, then why are you asking me? I mean, I could make up the answer and if I'm confident enough in my reply, then you're going to believe me. It's just a waste of time.

Furthermore, impacting the ability to randomly choose is the shape of the objects. Are they all the same size? Same type of object? You know what? I've got a better idea. Let's make it easy on ourselves. I'll call a couple of probability experts I know, and I'll get two independent answers for us to begin with right now.

9. "Provide an estimate for the number of goals in the Premier League."
Angela's Answer: Is that the name of the company doing the hiring? How many departments do — or will — they have? Oh, it's sports. I don't know. I don't do the sports thing.

10. "Tell me about your childhood."
Angela's Answer: You sure about that? Ain't nobody got time for that in an interview. Order my memoir and read it. It's called *Twinkle, a memoir*. Available on Amazon.com.

11. "No, really. Tell me about your childhood."
Angela's Answer: Look, we were on the run from the law. He was a bad man. Lot of bad…you know, this is getting me down.

12. "What are you hiding?"
    Angela's Answer: Hiding? I'm not hiding anything. I'm protecting you from a dark descent into your own soul that you don't have time for right now. I'm saving you from losing valuable work time. If. You're. Interested. Just read the book, damn it! When you get home. Otherwise…you know what, I'm not getting hired, am I?

Dancing at the Waffle House

No sense of humor at all: Bruce and Caitlyn bathroom doors.

Allen, Texas. Best known for...well, not sure what the town was known for in the past. But it made the news online in *The Daily Wire* when Dodie's Place Cajun Bar & Grill did a little bit of decorating in their back hall.

Screenshot from DailyWire.com

Dodie's is the place "Where All Your Friends Are!" What a friendly place. Lots of humor and laughing and food and such along with forty TVs on which to watch all four major sport groups.

Dancing at the Waffle House

Then the Pussy-Hat Wearing Politically Correct Democratic Liberal RINO Socialist Fascist Commies came to eat and the Texas Patty Melt hit the fan.

The P-HWPCDLRSFC [See pg. viii] said Dodie's was turning transgender women into a joke. The Dallas Morning News' Dom DiFurio saw the signs. He publicly said that the signs stigmatize transgenders and play to the area's conserva-tive audience, and that is why he felt he should report this story.

I call bull on Dom's reason.

Dom's a reporter. What do all reporters keep an eye out for? That's right. Stories. Dom saw the doors and said, "SuhWEET! Inflamma-tory story falls right into my lap. More public face time for *meeeeee. Thank you, Universe!"*

I say Dom thanked the Universe because I'm not sure if he believes in God or not and I wouldn't want to offend him by implying *that*, now would I?

Anyway, Dodie's was simply exercising their right to free speech and in no respect did they put up signage that made fun of Jenner or trans people. In fact, you saw the pictures above. Don't you agree that both the photos were excellent shots of each of Jenner's primes?

But that doesn't matter to the perpetually offended, and after Dom turned it into a *cause célèbre* Dodie's had to explain that they were only starting a discussion about the negative influence of political correctness.

What is amusing — and yet sadder — is that someone else said the great and awesome picture of Caitlyn Jenner was going to make other transgender women feel ugly because they weren't that far along in their process. Instead of celebrating the successful end of a long and torturous journey, they whine "She's too pretty and you're not."

And that statement, ladies and gentlemen, explains why the perpetually offended are nuts. Oops...did I just say that? Let me clarify.

It explains the psychosis of political correctness.

Dancing at the Waffle House

Dodie's Place Cajun Bar & Grill
November 2 at 5:53pm

First and foremost, our intention was not to make fun of or offend anyone when we installed the pictures of Bruce and Caitlyn on our bathroom doors. It was merely a lighthearted gesture to push back against the political correctness that seems to have a stranglehold on this country right now. We believe that political correctness has done more to silence rather than encourage important discussions that our society probably needs to have. Based on the mind-boggling feedback, both positive and negative, people are having that discussion. However, name calling and words like transphobic, deviant, racist, homophobic, bigot, etc. serve nothing but to continue to divide us instead of uniting us. After all, we are all part of the same race - the human race. Surely, we can discuss this topic and many others without slapping hurtful labels on each other. Please know that we are here to discuss this and move forward as a community. Everyone is welcome here.

👍 Like   💬 Comment   ↗ Share

490

27 Shares

View all 320 comments

Write a comment...

Dancing at the Waffle House

A widely shared meme from the Internets.

Dancing at the Waffle House

Fads and Fashion and Fat...Oh, brother.

I once read a book about how to pamper yourself and be all woman all the time because I deserved it... at least so said the authors who, of course, recommended all their products as a really good way to start on that project. I love the title. "A Year of Beauty and Health." Hahaha-duh-blah-blah-blah.

A year. I made it through one day. The methods were expensive, and I was broke and 19. The only method I could deploy was to shower and crawl into bed without drying off. Yep, that was one of the techniques. Yes, it was written by Beverly Sassoon and her husband, Vidal, with help from a real writer.

Money was no object for the soon-to-be-ex-wife of Vidal. Side note: My ex-husband used to work for Vidal out in California when he was first getting started. I attribute Vidal's success to how well my ex loaded Vidal's trucks. I contend that without my ex's attention to detail, product would have been mislaid and not made it to distributors and retailers on time.

You would think that Beverly could've shared some of her money later, but no, she acted like she didn't even know me. Bev has held up pretty good after all these years. I mean, her skin is crepey like a lot of old women's, but it doesn't look like she's overdone it on the plastic surgery or anything.

Moving on from that negative drama, when I was 22 I read a book by Adrien Arpel on how to look 10 years younger, but didn't do any of those things because I didn't want to look 12.

Dancing at the Waffle House

Adrien does not look good now. Lots of plastic surgery. I guess her suggested methods didn't work well after all. The older I got, the more practical I became. In my mid-30s I read a book about how to lose weight. Tactics and procedures to lose the poundage were burdensome, impractical, and expensive.

Implementing my genius as The Most Brilliant Woman In The World, I put my purse down before I got on the scale.

Ten pounds came off instantly.

See? Practical.

Works every time.

Dancing at the Waffle House

WE PAUSE FOR AN OVERT SALES PITCH

See book titles at front of book.

GIVE AS GIFTS TO YOUR FRIENDS!

Other People

"Other people are quite dreadful. The only possible society is one's self."
Oscar Wilde, "An Ideal Husband", 1895

"Who builds on the mob builds on sand."
Italian proverb

"The failure of one man is the fortune of another."
Francis Bacon, "Of Fortune", 1625

Dancing at the Waffle House

A Jazz Musician's OODA Loop.

As longtime readers know, Angela is a songwriter and, of late, turning into a singer who performs in front of total strangers who smile at and clap for her without getting paid or prompted. In fact, they pay for the privilege to hear her enabling her to pay for her supper.

This has been a hoot, but is not what this column is about, though it is connected.

This column is about OODA Loops. In military parlance, an OODA Loop is a quick succession of thought and action that defines the decision cycle when under fire. OODA stands for Observe, Orient, Decide, Act.

Specifically, this column is about OODA Loops as they are deployed in a Jazz musician's decision cycle. That is to say, how he will choose to whom he shall *give it good to* tonight.

There are several reasons Angela rarely wears dresses anymore. The main reason is that when Angela puts her gams on display, men tend to stutter, their eyes glaze over, and they can't walk straight. Yes, Angela knows her legs should be insured for a million dollars, but Angela cannot afford the premium.

Dancing at the Waffle House

Angela does not like her legs, has no clue why men react like that, and tends to think her gams are not so pretty. While Angela's ego sure does like men's reactions to them, Angela gets tired of not having conversations with men, so she wears pants.

Let's get back to the OODA Loop of the Jazz musician.

So there was Angela, going to be singing her new song *Crying Puddles* and, given the topic of the song, thought it would be appropriate to wear a dress that night to fit into the song and so Angela did, adding to that outfit hose and heels.

Waiting her turn to go onstage, Angela was sitting at the back bar at the venue when who walks by but Frank, not his real name.

Frank is a well-known Jazz musician who plays piano better than he plays drums though that has not stopped him from banging…on the drums. Angela has never been interested in Frank and Frank has always sensed that fact, if not flat-out known it, and has never tried to put the moves on Angela, for which she is grateful in the extreme.

But Frank has always only seen Angela in pants. That is to say, he has never seen a display of her gams and on this night, with Angela sitting at the bar on a tall chair and her legs crossed prettily, encased in suntan hose thus accentuating the positives even more, Frank walked by.

And there, in front of God and everybody, Frank perfectly executed a two-second OODA Loop. Here's how that happened.

Observed: Frank saw a pair of legs he liked.
Oriented: Frank immediately turned and headed toward the legs.
Decided: Frank looked up to see who owned the legs, saw Angela, and said to himself, "Oh, hell no."
Acted: Frank pivoted fast and walked away.

It was a perfect execution of a Jazz musician's OODA Loop.

Angela admired it so much that she immediately laughed aloud. Nobody knew why Angela was laughing. But, Angela knew what she was seeing and happily said to herself, "Column material!" She can't make this stuff up, y'all. She is a Citizen Reporter after all.

Practice makes perfect.

Let's be clear: Frank and Angela like each other perfectly fine as colleagues; conversation between the two happens. Six years ago, Frank once bragged to Angela that he sure gets lots of the good stuff because he is a "touring Jazz musician." That bored Angela. Frank understood immediately and never brought it up again.

He is not a stupid man.

And he doesn't like to waste time.

In any case, Frank has had many years to practice his OODA Loop technique and boy-oh-boy has it ever been perfected. But these days, Frank is in a bit of a quandary. One night here recently Frank was frank with Angela about his growing dissatisfaction with offers from firm-fleshed young women.

He sighed, "Angela, as you well know, I get offered the good stuff all the time. But now, when these young women offer to do me, well, I shudder. They are so...so...boring."

Frank recently turned fifty years old, and he talks about it all the time to get used to it. It's one thing to say, "I'm forty-nine." It is quite another to say, "I'm fifty."

Can Angela sympathize? She'll never tell.

He who would be fooled: Baby Doll is not amused.

"My ego is not tied up in my car," said the high-flying executive on the fast track in his company. "I could drive an old beater and it wouldn't bother me."

I simply nodded because how do you tell a man he has fooled himself? You can't. Well, you can, but it often doesn't work. Especially when he's jangling keys to his new and loaded-to-the-gills Benzie while pointing out the window wanting you to notice it.

I had hoped Tim (not even close to his real name) would get to the reason for our meeting, but he took my silence as a challenge. I didn't jump all over his statement like an eager acolyte rubber-stamping his "I'm one of the little people" attitude, so he felt compelled to keep talking about his ego and how unpretentious he was. He said he pretty much forced himself to drive a swanky car and wear swanky clothes and vacation in swanky spots and buy his wife swanky presents.

I nodded again and, for good measure, said as sincerely as possible, "Oh. Uh-huh. Yes."

This did not work and Tim (I'm not lying, this is not his real name) continued in his attempt to let me know he was on *my* level, not trying to lord it over me, no sir, he could drive an old car *just like me*, yes indeed. In fact, he was quitting all those — and here he lowered his head and confessed — *bad habits, you know....* Then he wiped at his nose and sniffed. Ah. Cocaine. That explained a lot about the progress of our recent projects.

Maybe Tim was prescient. Maybe he knew he wouldn't be keeping his job much longer and he was simply getting himself used to the idea of living lower on the hog. I believe he may have known because Tim was fired a few months later, along with his secretary.

Yeah, seems Tim and his wife, and his secretary and her husband, got kinky together. Not at the office. No, no, no. It was all off-premises...that anybody knew, of course. I mean, how do you prove a negative, right? But they were all using drugs and Tim was coming to work high and...it wasn't pretty.

Tim disappeared. I heard he moved to NOLA and got a job there, but I don't know. Can't find him on the Internet anywhere and for a high-flying mover and shaker always looking for his next job, you'd think he would at least be on LinkedIn.

If I could find Tim (I swear this is not his real name or even close though his real name does have two each of "i" and "l", an "a", "w", and "m") I would share with him some interesting statistics about the little people driving their cars longer. From a report by J.D. Power as reported in USA Today:

- The number of vehicles on the road that are at least 25 years old is about 14 million. That's up from about 8 million in 2002. Those are vehicles made in 1990 or earlier.
- Meanwhile, the number of vehicles that are 16 to 24 years old is 44 million. That's up from 26 million in 2002, according to IHSMarkit.com.

I am one of those people. Baby Doll, my faithful mare, is a 2002 Pontiac Bonneville who has recently gotten lots of new parts including an engine. Yes, doing that was cheaper than paying a monthly car payment for several years. And no, I didn't want to buy a used car and inherit somebody else's problems. I've looked after Baby Doll and she's looked after me. I plan to drive her until I die — barring anything catastrophic, of course.

Dancing at the Waffle House

Here is Baby Doll getting a new windscreen after she was brutally attacked on the highway when the vehicle in front threw a rock at her. Note her new front headlights.
She feels pretty! Oh, so pretty!

Numbers.

Did you know that 93 million people in this nation die every day from gun violence? That means our nation will be a wasteland in less than five days. When the edited snippet of the Virginia Governor Terry McAuliffe soundbite is pushed out, that's what unthinking people will think and believe.

Thank goodness we had a bold, fast-thinking reporter in the crowd who pointedly asked McAuliffe if he meant to say 93 ***million***? McAuliffe repeated that number then caught himself and said, "93 ***individuals*** a day." Still, according to the FBI, 93 is over double what the daily murder rate is, and since the FBI's stats include all forms of murder, death by gun is even lower. So McAuliffe still got it wrong.

Compared to most countries in this world, the US is extremely safe...and it isn't because of gun control. But the progressives do not care about truth. They care about revolutionary power grabs. That's why when Governor McAuliffe misspeaks, you won't see the Progressives, Democrats, RINOs, and the radical aging hippies say one thing about it.

But let President Trump misspeak and next thing you know they're screaming *LIAR!*

Dancing at the Waffle House

Liberals* are no fun, or The Case of T— and J. Brien.

Eliot Ness worked for the FBI for only six weeks.

"I cannot imagine Eliot Ness whining 'He's picking on me.' Or J. Edgar for that matter. I mean, I know J. Edgar liked his dresses and panties and bras, and he was a fanatic, but he went toe to toe even if his toes were inside his pink pumps."

Yes, I wrote that on Facebook in reply to a friend's post. Then her friend T—** said, "Hoover dressing in dresses is fake news." I replied, "You're just no fun at all."

See, if T— was any fun, he would've come back to me with something to carry the theme through, and together T— and I would have made some fake news of our own. Who knows?

T— could've said: "I heard J. Edgar liked to be called Jane Elinor at home."

At which point I could come back and say,

Dancing at the Waffle House

"Speaking of FBI Directors, I heard J. Brien likes his wife to spank him."

Then T— could say, "J. Brien likes spankings? Then why is he whining about Trump giving him one?"

I would reply: Hahahahaha! LOL for real.

Then T— would 👍.

    See how it works? Back and forth *fun*.
    But, no. T— just left that comment hanging and, gentlemen let me tell you, women don't like to be left hanging. T— didn't even try to defend himself against the charge of being a bore. How wussy is that?
    But I bet he's the guy behind you that honks his horn the millisecond red turns to green, passive-aggressive SOB that he is. I don't really know that about T—, but I can opine and surmise, can't I?
    Eliot Ness would never honk his horn that fast. He'd wait until you were ready. And Elliot would have some jokes to tell about his boss. And if Donald "The Hammer" Trump called him into a meeting, Eliot would sit at the table

Dancing at the Waffle House

in a confident manner, ask Donald to pass the salt, and would not be so scared he'd never had a meeting like that before that he wouldn't even think about writing extensive notes about it.

"Well, well, well...I...I...I...mean, that's just not how it's done here in D.C., so I was *skeert*," said J. Brien.

Liberals* are sucking the fun out of everything.

---

*Liberals are:
Those with "unearned moral superiority"***, wussy RINOs, power-hungry Socialists, RadFems and pussy-hat wearing celebrities and their blind-to-reality acolytes.

**Not his real initial.

***Attribution: Phrase stolen from a friend but I told him I was going to steal it and he didn't seem bothered by it.

FINAL NOTE: Eliot Ness worked for the FBI for only six weeks. Otherwise he was assigned to the Bureau of Prohibition where he assembled a group of eleven men called The Untouchables. They were first tasked with bringing down Al Capone. It was a bloody business. J. Brien would not have made the cut to join that group of manly men.

Dancing at the Waffle House

Lido Pimienta generates fake racism event so she doesn't have to pay for column inches.

I once knew a man who gave spiritual-based talks. Some might call him a preacher. He was a good speaker. Folks wanted to politely clap at the end to show their appreciation. But this man had a gimmick guaranteed to get them to think about him longer.

After each lesson he'd say, "Do not clap for me. Instead, bow your head in prayer and think about the lesson today. Talk to God about it. I am nothing. Merely an instrument and if you clap for me you will be worshiping a man, not God and that is just wrong."

He was so self-righteous about his nothingness that it came across as creepy. Of course, nobody clapped. Who wants to self-identify as a worshiper of a human when God is in the house?

Lido Pimienta, a proudly Brown female performer, also has a gimmick guaranteed to get people to think of her longer. She tells white audience members to move to the back rows and has all the Brown girls move to the front. But her gimmick is not what you think.

Pimienta wants you to believe she is all about level playing fields and access for all and so forth.

She isn't.

But we'll get to the real reason for her gimmick momentarily.

Pimienta says she's never had any trouble with getting white folk to move until she went to Halifax, Nova Scotia. Yes, Canada, that bastion of free healthcare and political correctness that all good Pussy-Hat Wearing Politically Correct Democratic Liberal RINO Socialist Fascist Commies in the US say is where they want to be but haven't moved yet.

Halifax did not give the result she wanted. Self-identified as an immigrant, Afro-Indigenous person, intersectional feminist, mother, and all of the other signifiers that qualify her as *Other*, Pimienta claimed overt racism from all whites in the audience if they merely stood closer to the stage than a black or Proudly Brown person.

Dancing at the Waffle House

Her great comment was that she didn't have time to waste with the white aggressive racists who were taking time out of her set. The scaredy-cat whiny-butt festival fell right in line with it, saying in a press release —

> We are going to try our best as a festival to create ways to make our spaces safer and more accessible for you. We hope we can rebuild some trust and that you will come back to our shows.

But there was no problem until Ms. Lido made one. Nobody was kept out. Everybody got a ticket. There were no safety issues. No fights in the audience. Everybody ready to hear some good music.

Until Pimienta deployed her gimmick to get free column inches in newspapers and online.

From DailyWire.com to Billboard.com to NationalPost.com, and more mainstream media outlets, Pimienta received massive amounts of free advertising and all she had to do was pose as a righteous, caring-more-than-you do-gooder who truly loves everything *other* — as long as it isn't a white human.

Dancing at the Waffle House

Lido demonstrates how to get free advertising.

Lido Pimienta Speaks
Out After Racism
Controversy at Halifax
Pop Explosion Festival

Billboard

2 days ago

Lido Pimienta Speaks
Out About "Overt
Racism" at Halifax Pop
Explosion

Exclaim!

2 days ago

Canadian Music
Festival Says Sorry For
'Racist' White Staffer
Who Didn't Want To...

The Daily Caller

3 days ago

Galileo Galilei: Dissing God or unmasking gods?

Galileo Galilei said faith is not truth. Was he dissing God when he dared to question the certainty of Church fathers' faith? In any case, their heads exploded.

We learned in school that Galileo dared to say the Earth was not the center of the Universe. Church leaders went on a full-out 15th century social media smear campaign against this man of faith.

Claiming he was teaching falsehoods and dissing God in the process, the Church declared an official Inquisitorial commission meant to shut down the debate once and for all time within those hallowed walls and around the world. In writing, mind you, they said that the Earth rotating around the Sun was —

"foolish and absurd in philosophy, and formally heretical since it explicitly contradicts in many places the sense of Holy Scripture" and that the idea of the Earth's movement "receives the same judgement in philosophy and...in regard to theological truth it is at least erroneous in faith".

In other words, ruin his reputation and then damn him, damn him to hell forever because he disagrees with us.
Us! The keepers and defenders of truth.
Us! The ones who are smarter than everybody else.
Us! Who know what the ignorant masses do not, cannot, and will never know or have hope to understand.

Dissing God?

But, there is one thing Galileo Galilei came to know: Faith of and by itself is not always the truth. After a time, nobody much thought about Galileo. But some, who did value truth, finally managed to have the Church's Inquisition ban formally lifted 359 years after condemning Galileo. The event was so huge, the announcement even made it to The New York Times — but only because it made the Church look bad. We chuckle at the naiveté of those ancients' faith. We shake our heads at the Church's ego trip. We say empirical scientific results rule. We point to Galileo as our proof.

However, Galileo's struggle — that is, convincing the powers-that-be they are wrong even when one can prove it — is alive and well in the most current Inquisition: Politically Correct Big Science against Real Data. Here's what's been happening for many years, and is only now publicly admitted:

Scientists are under pressure to produce quick results so that Product can be rolled out in order to make lots of money for investors who want to cash out as multi-gabillionaires after five years.

Fast results and big dollars.

How can fast results and big dollars come to be? That is easy.

First: Scientists report an R&D result based upon their belief they can't possibly be wrong. That is, they see what they want to and ignore what doesn't fit their narrative.

Second: Marketing massages the messaging: This is the new wonder product that will solve a Big Problem!

Third: Investors push their truth, convincing politicians to remove barriers to market. Trust us, they say, we aren't lying. See how sincere in our belief we are?

But BBC.com reports:

"Science is facing a 'reproducibility crisis' where more than two-thirds of researchers have tried and failed to reproduce another scientist's experiments. ...According to Edinburgh neuroscientist Prof Malcolm Macleod, 'The issue of replication goes to the heart of the scientific process.'...Scientific literature [has] been 'tidied up' to present a much clearer, more robust outcome."

I daresay financial and reputational pressure is being levied against higher-ups in the BBC, Professor Macleod, and all others documenting these findings about the nature of today's research. I bet there have been quiet discussions over friendly lunches with broad hints passed with the salt suggesting they remove themselves from this silly little path they're on or else dire consequences will follow.

Nothing I can do, old boy!
You can't say I didn't warn you.

Dancing at the Waffle House

How did the Middle Age Church fathers put it? Let's take their words and change them for today:

"Foolish and absurd to even question the results of the studies. To say we are wrong is simply heretical since we explicitly state you are contradicting our Holy Writ, The Study We Financed. The very idea that our approved scientists are wrong is ludicrous. You will not be allowed back in our hallowed halls if you persist in this. You shall be fired. No more funding dollars will come to you. Besides, admit it, you are wrong."

This new Inquisition applies not only to Big Pharma, but to those pushing the climate change agenda. Your Citizen Journalist has long said that something nasty is in the environmentalists' woodshed. Through the years, bits and pieces of information contrary to their findings have leaked out here and there.

Bits and pieces like 600 weather stations purposefully situated to gather distorted environmental impact data.

And Climategate.

And skewed global warming data.

And other measuring devices badly placed out of sheer stupidity.

Dancing at the Waffle House

And ginning up data where it doesn't exist. Has NOAA been caught red-handed? Oh dear.

The people reporting this got major pushback from around the world. But why do I, your Citizen Journalist and The Most Brilliant Woman In The World, believe them? Because of all the documentary proof of manipulation for nefarious means, and because those who claim their data to be correct use social and financial pressure to make others cave to their will.

Reminds me of Jeffrey Wigand, Kathryn Bolkovac, William Sanjour, Cate Jenkins, Philip Haney, the Thinthread Four, and other modern whistleblowers who defy the liars and the cheats and the powerful to tell the truth and diss self-appointed gods.

Galileo would have approved.

Dancing at the Waffle House

Dancing at the Waffle House

Dancing at the Waffle House

Angela K. Durden is a Citizen Journalist; songwriter; inventor of technology; crime novelist; general fiction novelist; and author of other books including children's, business, memoir, and works of humorous contemporary commentary on a variety of subjects.

More importantly, she is a woman on a spiritual journey. Her Heavenly Father has written the itinerary for this journey and has seen fit not to tell her anything about it as he rolls out one surprise stop after another.

Dancing at the Waffle House

Full comments by those who endorse this book:

If I were alive today, I would highly recommend you read this book by Angela K. Durden. It is no brag because it is fact that she is The Most Brilliant Woman In The World. I can say that because as The Most Brilliant Man in the World, at one time, I know excellent humor when I see it. Also, my good friends and faithful readers — Neal, Rush, and Sean — only wish they had the guts to write as she does. If I were alive today, I would be taking her on tour with me.

Oh, to see the faces of those ticked-off politicians and social justice warriors when they would hear her opine humorously. Damn, I hate it that I'm dead. But since I am, and the world has not had another humorist such as me since that plane crash, I nominate Angela K. Durden to take my place. I am sure you will agree.

Please give her your money as your ancestors once gave me theirs. You won't regret it.

Will Rogers
No longer bookable because he's dead,
but former highly paid actor, performer,
syndicated columnist, and expert lasso artist

Dancing at the Waffle House

I apologize to the reader of this book that I, Mark Twain, dead these many long years, have not been given more space to write back matter that matters. So, let me be quick for I shan't much have time to say it any other way in this short space:

The writings contained in these covers as written by my good friend Angela K. Durden — I would call her that if I were still alive — are a must read for all with any intelligence.

Just like the many books and articles I wrote through the years that most politicians publicly smiled at but privately railed against, and which mantle of humorous social commentary was taken up by Will Rogers after I died, Angela K. Durden is today ably filling that huge sucking void.

That is, she does a fine job of pointing out the foibles of those who take themselves so seriously they believe they have all the answers for everything and know better than you how to live your life.

Mark Twain
No longer writing because he's dead,
but former worldwide celebrity, writer,
columnist, author, novelist, and world traveler
who loved his wife and kids

Dancing at the Waffle House

In one of her many public statements, Angela K. Durden noted that the reason she can get away with saying what she does is because she is a Southern Woman who looks like a schoolteacher yet knows how to fake sincerity.

Prefacing her hard-hitting comments with words and phrases like Sweetie pie, Honey, Sugah, Bless your heart, and Oh, aren't you just the cutest thing ever, Durden throws people off guard with sweet words and smiles, and by giving them the feather because they aren't worth a whole bird.

Durden does not speak French, Spanish, or Greek, but she proves her love of multi-culturalism by uttering the phrases *Oui, oui, Monsieur*, *¡Ándale! ¡Ándale! ¡Arriba! ¡Arriba!*, and *Periménete, periménete, periménete … nai* when the time is right and the situation calls for it.

Angela K. Durden has been a humorist her entire life. Just ask her mother who always said, "You're joking, right?" or her ex-husband who is well known for saying to her "Oh, you think you're real funny, don't you?", and to friends and relatives who noted "She thinks she's a comedian." (And now you know one reason why he is the ex, though her mother still thinks she jokes.)

T.H. Smith
The Unknown Critic

Dancing at the Waffle House

Do you have your copy of these books? All are available on Amazon.com. See my Amazon.com Author page.

You know you need to order yourself one of each. Look, when you do that, that makes you a benefactor of the highest order. Heck, if you write me a letter (in care of my publisher) delivered by the U.S. Postal Service, I will reply and say, "Thank you very much for your support, you awesome person you!"

Angela K. Durden
C/O Blue Room Books
2425 Lawrenceville Highway #C7
Decatur, GA 30033

Dancing at the Waffle House

Dancing at the Waffle House

Dancing at the Waffle House

Dancing at the Waffle House

Dancing at the Waffle House

Dancing at the Waffle House

Excerpt from Whitfield, Nebraska

Available on Amazon.com: GET IT!

Autographed copy available from publisher.

Chapter 1: Meeting Headliner

In Whitfield, Nebraska, there are only three bars. And one of those is a strip joint.

I had arrived an hour ago. Was here on business and minding my own, sitting at the bar nursing a Crown and Coke. My back was to the stage while I enjoyed convivial conversation with the bartender. The headliner finished her last act and walked to the bar. Mama raised a gentleman, so I offered to buy her a drink, seeing as how she was so thirsty and all. Proper levels of hydration are often taken for granted and I didn't want to see this woman get any muscle cramps.

When she offered me the lap dance, I turned her down, like a proper gentleman would, you know, with a *No thank you, ma'am*, and a polite bob of the head. Four of her regular patrons took mighty big offense, though for the life of me I don't know why. And that's how I found myself flat on my back in a dirty alley, the IGA's back door ignoring me because I wasn't groceries to be unloaded, as four mad and drunk redneck types pounded on me. They weren't even taking turns. Headliner was screaming for help into a phone and before too very long a police car pulled up, siren screaming and one light flashing bright. Rednecks slowly scattered like rats who knew they would be back to finish the job when the lights went out.

    And that's how I found myself in the back of a cruiser with my face in Headliner's lap as she sweetly urged the cop, "Go faster, Baby Doll, faster!"

    Late next afternoon I checked myself out of the hospital, got in a taxi, and headed for Harvey's Chicken Strips and Chick Strippers, whose back door was good friends with IGA. Having left in a bit of a hurry the night before, my tab was unpaid. A gentleman honors his debts no matter how inconvenient. My car was still in the parking lot, both headlights busted out.

How did that happen? I distinctly remembered driving past the IGA with no mishaps, pulling into the side street without crashing into anything, and parking nose in to the building. Building didn't show any signs of damage. Both lights worked when I got there. I shrugged *que sera sera* and opened the trunk, slid a Slim Jim up my left sleeve and a thirty-eight Smith & Wesson into my back waistband. I might be honorable, but I wasn't stupid.

I opened the door, stepped in, and slid quick to the right, my back against the wall. A quick, but thorough, scan of the room showed my buddies from last night had not returned. Harvey stared at me and kept on shining that glass as I walked over and laid what I owed him on the bar and added ten twenties in a pile next to it. Harvey's seen it all, but he raised his eyebrows at that. In Whitfield, Nebraska, two hundred dollars is big money.

"What's that for?" he growled.

"This is what I owe you from last night," I said with one finger on the left pile, "and this,"

Dancing at the Waffle House

I put another finger on the twenties, "is for the party tonight."

"Who's invited?"

"Never did get around to filling out the guest list, but I'll know 'em when I see 'em."

Harvey pocketed the money. He didn't ring it up. What would Uncle Sam say about that? "Will you be wantin' chicken tonight? I got three dips to choose from."

"I won't be serving hors d'ouevres."

"No what?"

I translated using the local vernacular. "We won't be needin' no snacks."

"Oh." He paused. "Don't want no blood neither. Just painted the joint."

I looked at the twenty-five-year-old paint, scarred and beaten, then nodded at Harvey. I understood. And that's how I found myself sitting in the darkest corner of Harvey's Chicken Strips and Chick Strippers in Whitfield, Nebraska, the only strip club for two hundred square, flat miles. I took this time to get a quick nap; hospitals aren't restful places. Thanks to Headliner's quick call, the damage to my body was livable. Nothing broken, nothing missing, all the pertinent parts still worked, at least the ones I'd had opportunity to check out. I've had worse.

"Wake up!" Officer Baby Doll kicked my feet. "Why are you still in town?"

Always did want to deliver this line, so I gave it my best offhand smartass interpretation when the opportunity arose. "Ah, officer, catching up on my beauty sleep, but I seem to keep on gettin' interrupted."

"Not funny," Baby Doll said. "You better not stir up no more trouble."

"I didn't stir it up last night," I smiled, gently protesting my innocence.

The best hackneyed screenwriter in Hollywood couldn't have written better lines than what came out of his mouth. "Don't get cute with me, smartass. You better watch out. If it wasn't for Verleene, you'd be in the pokey" — yes, he said pokey, I'd swear on my sainted mother's grave except she isn't dead — "right about now. From now on you best be showin' your gratefulness to that little lady and don't be dissin' her none. She's a respected member of this here community. She's been more helpful to all levels of law enforcement than you will ever know."

Ah. Verleene. That must be Headliner. "I'm sure she has. Give respect. Noted for future reference. Thank you for your concern, Ba-, ummm, Officer."

Officer Baby Doll stared for one last minute and I don't mean a metaphorical full minute, finally grunted and walked out. I closed my eyes, shut out the stink of the stale odors of last night's sweaty strippers and fried chicken, and resumed my wait. Harvey heard my guests arriving in the parking lot before I did.

"Wake up. Your guests are here. 'Member whut I said. No blood."

"Thanks, Harvey. As far as it depends upon me, I will be peaceable with all men."

"What"?

"I won't spill blood unless I'm forced to."

"Oh. Okay."

Harvey's eyes went to the door. My eyes closed. Didn't need them quite yet seeing as how my ears told me all I needed to know. I heard the door slam open. Four men shuffled in like rats, bodies heavy, not graceful, and surely not light on their feet even though they had been dancing on me the night before. The door closed and the footsteps stopped. They were mouth breathers and I heard the bones grinding in their thick ex-high-school football player necks as they looked from me, back and forth to each other, and finally to Harvey. I wondered if the town had a chiropractor.

Harvey let me know who the ringleader was. "Your regular, Tater?"

Go to Amazon.com to order the book so you can read the rest. You won't be sorry.

Dancing at the Waffle House

DANCING AT THE WAFFLE HOUSE
© 2018 All Rights Reserved
978-0-9854623-3-8
Imprint: Blue Room Books
Angela K. Durden
angeladurden@msn.com